Anomaly

John C. Woodcock

ISBN: 1535013001
ISBN-13: 978-1535013000

CONTENTS

ACKNOWLEDGMENTS

1. Cover Image: *Dust Devil*. NASA: Public Domain.

2. Image: *A Pair of Shoes*. Vincent van Gogh: Public Domain.

P REFACE TO 2nd EDITION

It is now 2025. The global effort to erase any access to the living psyche is almost complete. Decades ago I had a dream in which

> I am sitting with the Pope and the American Archbishop. I am talking animatedly with the Bishop about Materialism, reaching its end. 'It's taken its time', he said. I agreed and said that it must be lived through to the end before something else can come through. I was charged with a fire that suffused my face which glowed. The Bishop got caught up in our discussion interrupting me but the Pope saw that I was infused with a spiritual fire and leaned over to his Bishop and said in a soft voice in Latin, to listen, stay quiet, don't stop me from talking. I somehow understood ... we sat in the silence. He watched me carefully, my face glowing softly, then his eyes rolled back and he said some more in Latin that I could not catch. A soft fire had suffused my face in a soft glow in my animation. Pope Paul was watching me closely. He saw something.

I had this dream in 1995 and its truth is now manifestly visible in the postmodern world.

Materialism is now reaching into our "inner" lives to the degree that access to the living psyche is denied. Dreams are now addressed in the same style that we address outer objects—as utterly alien to us, having nothing to do with us psychologically. More sensitive individuals are having apocalyptic dreams but in the sense of a cinema presentation to the dreamer. Upon waking the dreamer remains untouched, unmoved, shaking it off with a shrug.

Dreams no longer can penetrate consciousness

which has hardened, even petrified. We are alienated from the waters of the living psyche! Under these catastrophic conditions, how does the living psyche respond? Our shutting the psyche out is a cultural move to which the psyche has a response. It seems to me there are two discernible *movements*.

The living psyche may very well withdraw, plunging us into a nightmarish darkness of spirit, as I have written extensively about in my book Light Withdrawn. This soul movement is succinctly expressed in this poem:

When the Light of an Era Goes Out

what does it mean
if the light is going out
it means it's over
it's done with
it's gone
the light has gone out
it's over
it's gone
the light is gone
the light of this civilization is gone

it's not coming back

Llewellyn Vaughan-Lee

The second discernible *movement* of psyche constitutes the theme of this book. The living psyche is violently breaking into waking consciousness in the form of anomalies—real intrusive events that cannot be understood in terms of the logic of materialism.

I begin Part One with an essay describing where we

have arrived in terms of language and cultural practices that effectively erase any access to the living psyche.

C. G. Jung had discovered and devoted his life's work to the reality of the objective psyche. Since his death in 1961, the cultural move away from psyche as a reality has become the hallmark of philosophy, psychology, and most other disciplines.

When technology was invented to scan the human brain, this move accelerated dramatically and the first essay Psyche in Oblivion explores the almost universal denial of the reality of psyche in the "official narratives" of our Western culture. The psyche, as a reality, is now in oblivion. What counts as knowledge no longer makes any reference to psyche. Yet, because psychic reality is *reality*, there are consequences to ignoring it, and some individuals, such as Tom Wolfe, are letting us know just what they are.

Subsequent essays in Part One show how the claims of the living psyche are becoming visible as the inward necessity of many contemporary cultural phenomena. This necessity shows up as anomalies in a variety of cultural disciplines to the discerning inner eye. In Part Two I focus on the intrusive invisible appearance of the living psyche as the "within" of various cinematic forms.

PART ONE

PSYCHE IN OBLIVION

The ever-astute educator, George Orwell, in his famous little book, 1984, exposes the intimate connection between language and psyche (or its demise) this way:

> It's a beautiful thing, the destruction of words. Of course the great wastage is in the verbs and adjectives, but there are hundreds of nouns that can be got rid of as well ... You haven't a real appreciation of Newspeak, Winston," he said almost sadly ... "Don't you see that the whole aim of Newspeak is to narrow the range of thought? In the end we shall make thought crime literally impossible, because there will be no words in which to express it. Every concept that can ever be needed, will be expressed by exactly one word, with its meaning rigidly defined and all its subsidiary meanings rubbed out and forgotten.[1]

Any writer like me who bases his entire body of work on the reality of psyche would be wise to comprehend and come to terms with the prevailing attitude of complete denial of psyche—often dismissed as the god of the gaps, i.e. an unnecessary obfuscating concept used when we have a temporary lack of empirical knowledge.

In 2007, TIME magazine published a special edition on the brain: The Mystery of Consciousness.[21] Various experts in the fields of brain research and consciousness were interviewed and so the articles explored the latest findings, theories, and difficulties surrounding the "mind-body" problem, or how consciousness and the brain are related. Much of the discussion focuses on the scientific breakthroughs made possible by MRI scans of the brain. Further discussions use the amassing body of evidence from these increasingly sensitive and precise measurements in order to develop theories of consciousness, or mind, or us as seemingly self-aware beings.

These articles, though not comprehensive or exhaustive, and intended for a general audience, do show the emergence of a growing consensus amongst foremost researchers concerning the nature and provenance of consciousness, and therefore us as mental beings. We are in the process of forming a new set of collective representations about us and our bodies, and this set is taking hold of our imaginations fast (if I may use that word any more—and there is doubt that I will be able to). We are quickly becoming accustomed or habituated to seeing ourselves a certain way and we may soon *become* that certain way.

MRI scans, along with more invasive investigations, show conclusively how much consciousness and the brain are tied together, to use a loose term for a moment. As Steven Pinker says, "... consciousness can be pushed around by physical manipulations." He cites electrical stimulation, chemicals, and radical surgeries, as examples of interventions that manipulate consciousness. Physical death means as far as anyone can know, death of consciousness. Even out-of-body experiences can be manipulated by stimulating the appropriate areas of the brain. Every activity of consciousness is rapidly associated with a physical area of the brain, to the extent that Pinker can claim that, "cognitive scientists can almost read people's thoughts from the blood flow in their brains."[3]

From these incontestable facts a dominant theory has emerged: consciousness is an emergent property of biology! All experts cited by Pinker in his article share this theory—Colin McGinn: "Nevertheless, consciousness is surely a natural biological product as devoid of the otherworldly as digestion ... "; Michael Gazzaniga: "Consciousness is an emergent property and not a process in and of itself. Our cognitive capacities reflect distributed processes throughout the brain"; Bernard Baars: "The topic of consciousness is much like sex in the Victorian age. Scientifically sex is just another part of biology..."; Antonio Damasio: "All the natural history required to understand consciousness is now readily available in evolutionary biology and psychology"; Daniel Dennett, as paraphrased by Pinker: "Anything you would do to understand consciousness—like finding out what wavelengths make people see green ... boils down to information processing in the brain ... "[4]

The theory of mental process emerging from physical ones has of course been around before brain research really accelerated with MRI technology but now it seems universally accepted amongst experts, almost a habit of thought, a common sense starting point to all further examination of consciousness and its relation to the brain. Thus, we are collectively thinking of ourselves (our consciousness thinking about itself and its origins) as biological products, our provenance lies exclusively in the physical or biological domains. Therefore, the processes of biology are the processes of consciousness. For example, when biological processes come to an end so does consciousness. If biological processes are determined by evolutionary principles such as survival, adaptation, competition etc., then so is consciousness. This way of thinking about others and ourselves is thus becoming a collective representation and for many people it is already so.

Although Pinker gives greatest weight to these researchers of the brain and its processes, he does give a nod to an understandable hesitation on the part of many "nonscientists" to think of themselves that way. But Pinker's nod is only for the sake of an easy dismissal of such complaints. He says for example that some people (apparently not worth naming alongside the experts that he is aligned with) see the Hard

Problem of consciousness as an opportunity to "sneak the psyche back in." Note the pejorative term "sneak."

These anonymous people are sneaky. He dismisses such attempts as nothing more than a renaming of the Hard Problem: the mystery of consciousness becomes the mystery of the psyche and we are none the wiser. In this kind of easy dismissal Pinker joins the official narrative which eschews any version of a god of the gaps i.e. any attempt to fill our present gaps in knowledge with an unnecessary obfuscating term like god, or psyche, or similar untestable idea. Instead he shows his allegiance to an unassailable optimism of modern researchers. As Colin McGinn puts it, "why is it (consciousness) so hard to tame scientifically? The answer, I suggest, lies not in the stars (god of the gaps), but in ourselves; our brains have not evolved with the necessary equipment to resolve this mystery."[5]

We can hear the resounding optimistic "yet" coursing through his argument. We don't need god because we only have to wait until our brains or our knowledge can fill in those temporary gaps. In a small token of recognition Pinker mentions one (and only one) author who holds arguments counter to the prevailing one that he, Pinker and a host of others hold dearly. But he does so only to dismiss it again, almost casually as if the counter argument does not even really warrant such a waste of ink. The author is Tom Wolfe who wrote an essay: Sorry, but Your Psyche Just Died. Wolfe's essay may be seen as succinct summary and critique of the new neurosciences and their theoretical forays into the theory of consciousness. He begins with:

> Brain imaging was invented for medical diagnosis. But
> its far greater importance is that it may very well
> confirm, in ways too precise to be disputed, certain
> theories about "the mind," "the self," "the psyche,"
> and "free will" that are already devoutly believed by
> scholars in what is now the hottest field in the
> academic world, neuroscience.[6]

He goes on to identify the central issue that
neuroscience is concerned with today:

> We now live in an age in which science is a court from
> which there is no appeal. And the issue this time
> around, at the end of the twentieth century, is not the
> evolution of the species, which can seem a remote
> business, but the nature of our own precious inner
> selves.[7]

He addresses the same theory of consciousness that
Pinker espouses in his article: the theory that asserts
consciousness is a product of brain processes. He
examines the rippling effect of this theory out from the
specialty of neuroscience into the wider worlds of
politics, psychiatry, education, sociology, and so on. He
gives many examples of the consequences when we
begin to regard one another as pre-determined
biological entities in all respects. That is to say, Wolfe
provides us with an early glimpse of what lies in store
for us if the dominant theory of consciousness
provided by neuroscience becomes a collective
representation:

> Eventually, as brain imaging is refined, the picture may
> become as clear and complete as those see-through
> exhibitions, at auto shows, of the inner workings of
> the internal combustion engine. At that point it may

become obvious to everyone that all we are looking at is a piece of machinery, an analogy chemical computer, that processes information from the environment. "All," since you can look and look and you will not find any ghostly self inside, or any mind, or any psyche. …

Thereupon, in the year 2006 or 2026, some new Nietzsche will step forward to announce: "The self is dead"—except that being prone to the poetic, like Nietzsche, he will probably say: "The psyche is dead." He will say that he is merely bringing the news, the news of the greatest event of the millennium: "The psyche, that last refuge of values, is dead, because educated people no longer believe it exists." Unless the assurances of the Wilsons and the Dennetts and the Dawkinses also start rippling out, the lurid carnival that will ensue may make the phrase "the total eclipse of all values" seem tame.[8]

Wolfe ends with an apocalyptic vision of science finally turning on itself with its own skepticism:

I suddenly had a picture of the entire astonishing edifice collapsing and modern man plunging headlong back into the primordial ooze. He's floundering, sloshing about, gulping for air, frantically treading ooze, when he feels something huge and smooth swim beneath him and boost him up, like some almighty dolphin. He can't see it, but he's much impressed. He names it God.[9]

That may be but Pinker acknowledges none of Wolfe's examples and counter arguments. He off-handedly dismisses the entire essay with the comment that Wolfe has it backwards, that biology offers a far sounder basis for morality that Wolfe's "unproven dogma of an immortal psyche". Far from agreeing with

Wolfe's prognosis of a future in which the phrase "the total collapse of values" will seem tame, Pinker offers what seems to me a naïve argument in an attempt to gain further support for his own dogma of biology first, consciousness second. In so doing he inadvertently invokes a word that has long belonged to the domain of the psyche: He says:

Yet once we realize that our own consciousness is a product of our brains and that other people have brains like ours, a denial of other people's sentience becomes ludicrous ... The undeniable fact that we are all made of the same flesh makes it impossible to deny our common capacity to *suffer* (my emphasis).[10]

Wolfe went to considerable trouble in his essay, the same one that Pinker dismisses, to demonstrate that, in *fact*, a term Pinker loves, people are not behaving the way Pinker wishes they would, when they learn about their biological pre-determinism. On the contrary they are coming up with ways to dehumanize one another with alarming frequency:

The male of the human species is genetically hardwired to be polygamous, i.e., unfaithful to his legal mate. Any magazine–reading male gets the picture soon enough. (Three million years of evolution made me do it!) Women lust after male celebrities, because they are genetically hardwired to sense that alpha males will take better care of their offspring. (I'm just a lifeguard in the gene pool, honey.) Teenage girls are genetically hardwired to be promiscuous and are as helpless to stop themselves as dogs in the park. (The school provides the condoms.) Most murders are the result of genetically hardwired compulsions. (Convicts can read, too, and they report to the prison psychiatrist: "Something came over me... and then the knife went in".)[11]

Somehow Pinker's sunny theory of the genesis of morality sinks into the morass when confronted with such undeniable facts! Pinker is quick to identify and eschew Wolfe's "dogma" of an immortal psyche but it does seem easy to identify the other fellow's dogma while remaining blind to one's own. The theory of consciousness that states that consciousness emerges from matter persists in the face of a difficulty that is recognized by neuroscience as a formidable one.

How DO physical processes lead to mental ones? Neuroscience has no answer but blithely proceeds anyway on the optimistic basis that, if not now, we soon will know (no god of the gaps, remember). So this difficulty, far from being seen as an insurmountable obstacle to the theory, is simply set aside as more evidence amasses, showing an indubitable connection between mental and physical states. In other words, when a possible contraindication to the theory arises, it is simply put aside and the theory proceeds unmodified in any way. As Colin McGinn says:

> The paradox of the mind-body problem is that the explanatory causes of consciousness in the brain are not discoverable by inspecting the brain, and introspection cannot reveal the rootedness of consciousness in brain tissue ... Nevertheless, consciousness is surely a natural biological product ...[12]

Right from the outset, conceptual difficulties are announced and then dismissed. Only those findings that support the theory are let in. Nothing can challenge such a "theory" which appears more and more like, well, a dogma. Once such a habit of thought is entrenched it tends to assimilate new facts to itself and excludes any facts that challenge it. I think we can observe this process in the current "theory" of consciousness.

If a dogmatic point of view is holding people in thrall we may gain some insight into the phenomenon by studying its history. There is famous example of the early 20th century which illustrates this habit of thought and its power to enthrall: Freud's theory of seduction. He made a pioneering step of examining (unconscious) mental states in order to find causes for otherwise inexplicable physical states (such as hysterical blindness etc.)

Freud could not accept what his own clinical expertise was telling him. Mental states are "causing" physical ones, i.e. the mental state is prior, and the physical is secondary. Instead, his theory of neurosis and his developmental theory posit a physical cause prior to the observed mental state, which admittedly is still prior to the physical symptom in the adult. At first he proposed concrete sexual assault on the child as the physical cause.

This step alienated him professionally for many years so he tried another form of the seduction theory which spoke of sexual fantasy (his version of the oedipal myth for example) that lies darkly in the child's unconscious mind. This theory seems at first to be friendlier to the view that mental states can be ontologically prior to physical ones, until we read his account of how these childhood fantasies come about:

> In inquiring into the origin of incest dread it could be expected that here also is the choice between possible

explanations of a sociological, biological, and psychological nature in which the psychological motives might have to be considered as representative of biological forces.

He then appeals to Darwin's explanation, which he calls an historic explanation.

Drawing from current studies of apes and believing Darwin's account of the origin of mankind, Freud concocts a story of the genesis of the incest taboo:

> Let us now envisage the scene of such a totem meal and let us embellish it further with a few probable features that could not be adequately considered before ... One day the expelled brothers ... slew and ate the father ... Of course these cannibal savages ate their victim ... the totem feast, which is perhaps mankind's first celebration, would be the repetition and commemoration of this memorable criminal act, with which so many things began, social organization, moral restrictions and religion.[13]

When Freud could no longer locate the cause of adult neurosis in physical childhood trauma he reached into the deep past, armed with Darwin's vision of our biological evolution, and "found" a physical trauma which could cause the mental state of the neurotic (presence of forbidden desires etc.) Like modern neuroscience, Freud proposed his theory and made the facts fit, ignoring other equally plausible theories such as the one that could have accounted easily for his clinical findings that show mental states are prior to physical ones. Again, like modern neuroscience, theoretical distortions are introduced and then ignored so that the dogma may succeed. For example, how can a physical trauma putatively occurring millennia ago affect the mental state of a modern person? Freud's answer is through the mechanism of inherited memory. But how well can a concept of inherited memory (a mental state) fit with a purely biological account of our origins?

We can go even further back than Freud, before Darwin, and discover that a movement towards the dogma of "physical first, then mental" was emerging in the use of language, following Descartes' famous distinction between material objects of the world and the immaterial subject (consciousness). This division immediately caused problems since animals and plants were placed on the side of matter yet they were clearly different from rocks and minerals. A further division had to occur between animate matter and inanimate matter in the late 18th century.

Prior to the Cartesian division, matter was experienced as an indivisible whole called life, or even existence. Material existence had both a mental and physical aspect. Our ancestors did not think about those aspects in the way of opposites, as we do today. The later division into animate and inanimate matter, or as we would say today, living tissue and corpse, is a very uncomfortable one that has led to the predicament of neuroscience, which is forced to ask the contorted question: how does a mental state arise from living tissue?

The answer is embedded, unexamined in the question—living tissue! The concept of *living* tissue can only mean a reference to a totality of mental and physical states, or else the word "living" means next to nothing, as C.S. Lewis has shown so eloquently.[14]

Scientists who worried about how mental states can possibly emerge from purely physical processes seem to be asking how a mental state arises from something that is already a unity of mental and physical states i.e. living tissue. The only way to resolve this conceptual tangle is by examining the history of the division between mental and physical states and seeing how the division was forced with many people feeling the strain and ultimately becomes an impossible one unless of course we are prepared to abandon the fullness of the word Life altogether by reducing it to a mere abstraction.

Now we are at the point where we can inquire if there might be discernible movement within the dogma that we are biological entities only possessing an emergent property called consciousness with its quality of fleetingness ("a maelstrom of events distributed across the brain").[15] As I have shown, this dogma is strengthening even in the face of conceptual confusion and dismissal of any counter arguments or contrary facts. To put it another way, if a habit of thought is in ascendancy, what gives it strength and endurance, if not reason and argument?

I think there is a discernible movement within the debate and I think that it is this movement that is providing the energy (I better not say "life") to the dogma. This is where we come to Newspeak.

According to Pinker the least controversial feature of the problem of consciousness according to neuroscience is "the idea that our thoughts, sensations, joys and aches consist entirely of physiological activity in the tissues of the brain. Consciousness does not reside in an ethereal psyche that uses the brain like a

PDA; consciousness is the activity of the brain."[16] This is a succinct expression of the dogma. Within this expression is a clear dismissal of words such as "psyche" as having any reference beyond a material one.

Modern theories can and do become collective representations. Newton's theory of gravity is a good example. We now perceive objects falling passively subject to gravitational forces whereas once they were perceived as eagerly seeking (falling or rising) their desire's fulfillment or natural place relative to the centre of the universe. Words purportedly having an intangible reference now have no place in the new dogma and will be taken out of the theoretical language altogether. Here is an example of the Newspeak that is already in place. Keep in mind that the speaker is talking about you and me, and indeed, himself:

"We dream in order to forget." ... the brain is like a machine that gets in the groove of connecting its data in certain ways (obsessing or defending or retaining), and that those thinking pathways might not be the most useful for us. But, when we sleep, the brain fires much more randomly. And it is this random scouring for new connections that allows us to loosen certain pathways and create new, potentially useful, ones. Dreaming is a shuffling of old connections that allows us to keep the important connections and erase the inefficient links. A good analogy here is the defragmentation of a computer's hard drive: Dreams are a reordering of connections to streamline the system.[17]

Nowhere to be seen is the pronoun "I". We now use "brain-mind". Even the word "interpret" which refers to an intangible mental process is in quotes to show that we must read it as an "as if." For scientists such as

Francis Crick (who is quoted in the above passage), dreams hold no meaning at all and simply function to remove unwanted memories. There are of course resistance movements to this theory of dreams as well as to the dismissal of psyche, imagination, self, and a host of other words referring to intangible meaning but they pale before the onslaught of MRI scans and the avalanche of evidence showing that just about every mental state is tied to some aspect of the brain.

A theory transitions to a collective representation when ordinary people begin to think of themselves and others in the way the dogma describes, i.e., as brains and stimuli. This thinking slips into the unconscious (should I say "automatic"?) functioning and we begin to perceive the world that way. Far from Pinker's belief that deep knowledge of our biological roots will open the door to deeper empathy of our neighbour's suffering, we face the prospect of a world of brains bumping against other brains. To gain a vivid glimpse of such a world I can think of no better example than C.S. Lewis' book, That Hideous Strength. Perhaps a passage from that sublime fiction will give the flavour of what may await us if the dominant theory of consciousness becomes a collective representation:

> If you reflect for a moment, said Frost, you will see that your question has no meaning except on the level of the crudest popular thought. Friendship is a chemical phenomenon; so is hatred. Both of them presuppose organisms of our own type. The first step towards intercourse with the macrobes is the realisation that one must go outside the whole world of our subjective emotions. It is only as you begin to do so that you discover how much of what you

mistook for your thoughts was merely a by-product of your blood and nervous tissues ... You are to conceive the species as an animal which has discovered how to simplify nutrition and locomotion to such a point that the old complex organs and the old body that contained them are no longer necessary. That large body is therefore to disappear. Only a tenth part of it will be needed to support the brain. The individual is to become all head. The human race is to become all Technocracy.[18]

There are some hopeful signs, from within the field of neuroscience, where the dogma is held a little at arm's length. Some concessions are being made towards the mystery of consciousness and its relationship with matter. In the same TIME magazine edition, dedicated to the brain, there is an essay by Scott Haig M.D. It is a sensitive but unsparing portrayal of the last days of a man with terminal cancer that had invaded his brain, replacing much of it with tumour tissue.

Against all expectations, his consciousness returned briefly and he could say his goodbyes. Haig was shocked because as a physician he knew the brain just could not be functioning in a way to support speech or even coherence—as he says, "Where that gray stuff grows (the tumour), the brain is just not there." Yet, the patient spoke coherently to his family before dying.

Haig goes on to theorize:

The mind is a uniquely personal domain of thought, dreams, and countless other things, like the will, faith and hope. These fine things are as real as rocks and water, but, like the mind, weightless and invisible, maybe even timeless.[19]

Such brave assertions in the face of the dogma may

not be enough to alter the collective representations of the future, maybe not enough to avert Lewis' or Wolfe's glimpse of possible futures, but they are enough to stir the hearts of other resonant psyches and that is where I find a realistic hope of a different future from the one offered by the dogma. But how can such a different future arise and find its way into public discourse, finally becoming a collective representation?

In my book, Transformation of the World, I outline the sequence of steps that transform the participation of an individual with "possible futures" into a collective representation, or shared cultural practice:

a) The individual effort in which an individual's imagination experiences an aspect of an emerging future;

b) The individual becomes a mouthpiece of this future (artist, teacher, author, leader, etc.);

c) The willingness on the part of others to see the future the same way the individual does (e.g. by accepting an artist's work);

d) Through habit, the group's perception becomes the contours of a new world.[20]

We can see this sequence appearing in connection with the dogma I describe above: Darwin gives us his picture of our origins, i.e., the material world appears first, then consciousness as a late product of matter. Many take up his picture of the emergence of consciousness from matter and enshrine it in our educational system etc.

Now this picture is so habitually accepted that we have come to perceive the world that way—as a material object that somehow produced human consciousness as an epiphenomenon or emergent property.

There are many authors, artists etc. who, like Thomas Wolfe and C.S. Lewis, give us a glimpse of what horrors await us if the dogma succeeds in becoming a collective representation. Since we are still in a time of transition, or as some would say, chaos, we are in a position to ask if there are other possible futures emerging in the imagination of individuals which could also become a collective representation of ourselves and of the world. In fact there are many and we can get a good sense of this by watching the mass media in which there is an uncompromising war going on in the domain of competing ideas of our future.

It is taking place mainly in politics and economics since power and money are the engines driving our choices today. There is no more dialogue, thoughtful discussion, or conversation among people today in these domains. Instead we find a "winner takes all" competition in which participants strive to define the issue their way and to eliminate alternative voices as quickly and brutally as possible.

I see in this pervasive dogfight of competing narratives an accelerating competition between individuals each seeking to influence the next set of collective representations. We all seem to believe that individuals can make a decisive contribution to the formation of our future, in flagrant contradiction to the prevailing picture of evolution which describes the emerging future with no reference to the actions of individuals at all—it's all driven by DNA, the dogma claims.

But the domains of money and power come into

play at Step 2 of the sequence I outlined above. To get a glimpse of other emerging possible futures we need to explore Step 1 a little more closely. Where are these combatants in the media getting their ideas? To be sure, many are getting their ideas from someone else (Step 2) but a few are developing their ideas from within their own imagination (Step 1).

It is not easy to trace ideas circulating in the market place back to the individuals who "gave birth" to the idea, but it is possible. In fact I have done so in the case of two ideas that rather quickly became collective representations, one in the world of public relations and the other in the world of mathematics and computer science.[21] In each case we can relatively easily see how an original experience in the imagination of an individual is taken up by others and quickly becomes a habit of thought and then a commonly perceived reality.

THE LIGHT WITHIN OUR EVER DARKENING SHADOW

Two real empirical events in the world: a debate on the Iran Nuclear Deal and Donald Trump's candidacy for President of the USA. In each case I felt the resonating feeling that I spoke of in the Introduction. My ordinary discursive writing suddenly shifted into another style altogether. The disjunction between these "outer events" and an "inner" one—a dream—collapsed. You could call what followed a kind of *poesis*, and something new was revealed to me. I simply let it flow as I wrote it down. Emerging from within these events in the world, once reflected in my mind, was a new thinking, one that unites turbulence or chaos, with stillness—this is a hint of the character of the new appearances ...

... the horror ... the horror!

Col. Kurtz in "Apocalypse Now!"

In 1948, three years after the Atomic Bomb dropped on Hiroshima and Nagasaki, Jung spoke to a man who had worked on the Manhattan project. Jung asked him whether the whole Earth could now be destroyed. When he learned that it could, "Jung sat focused, having listened closely to each word, absorbing. Suddenly he lifted his hands and smote his left palm with his right fist, saying, 'Good!' with finality. Somehow the subject was settled, and we never had any further explanation of what he may have meant."[22]

I do not know if Jung, or anyone close to him, subsequently elaborated on this provocative declaration but given what we know about the supreme importance Jung placed on the psychology of the shadow, we can speculate about his meaning. I believe that Jung thought that the shock of the atomic bomb, bursting into consciousness and the world stage, would surely bring about a reappraisal of the danger in neglecting the shadow as a psychological reality.

The darkness we see in the world, as events like the atomic bomb, is also psychological darkness and psychologist Jung favored the cultural practice of "integrating the shadow". This work would produce an individual who "knows that whatever is wrong in the world is in himself, and if he only learns to deal with his own shadow he has done something real for the world. He has succeeded in shouldering at least an infinitesimal part of the gigantic, unsolved social problems of our day".[23]

Whether or not Jung had this aspiration in mind when he declared "Good!", we know that, sixty-five years on, the darkness in the world has increased exponentially and the importance of the humble practice of "integrating the shadow" has diminished almost to nothing. Jung understood that "the darkness in the world is perpetuated and deepened through the agency of human beings who do not see their own darkness—the darkness within that we carry in all our actions in the real world."[24] In other words, human beings who do not perceive the outer darkness also as an "inner" psychic factor today perpetuate the darkness in the world.

Since Jung's time there is no sign that "shadow work" as a cultural practice has any currency in our understanding of, or dealings with the enormous social problems today. "Shadow work" is an example of what Heidegger calls a marginal cultural practice. A cultural practice is a *way of being*, for an individual or group, that organizes activities so that the things of the world appear to the practitioners in a particular way, for the sake of a "future" meaning, towards which the practice aims. For example, taking a walk through the mountains with a geologist opens one's eyes to fresh appearances.

The same mountains that appeared to the naïve mind as a jumble of rocks, now come alive as residues of past earthquakes, volcanic action, vast seas, violent upheavals in the earth's crust—all revealed in the twisted layers of various forms of rocks—now rendered visible, thanks to the practice and language of geology.

Shadow work is also a cultural practice, with its peculiar language and correlative appearances, now marginalized almost to extinction, since Jung's time. The things rendered "visible" to the practitioner of shadow work are *psychic phenomena*, i.e. those real phenomena in the world that appear with depth, meaning, truth, and consciousness, each revealing the whole within its particularity. Today, these real appearances are inextricably contained within language, or, better, constitute the very within-ness of language, when language is experienced as a psychic phenomenon. I'll give an example of how such (linguistic or psychic) phenomena can appear to the practitioner of shadow work.

I recently watched a debate on the issue of the Iran nuclear deal. It didn't take long before tempers flared and attacks were launched across the moderator's chair. In terms of language, the content remained exclusively political, military, ideological, and economic. These are, after all, the major forms of rhetoric in use today. While remaining within these narratives, the debaters became increasingly emotional and strident. At no point, however, did this emotionality rise to the level of content of the debate.

No one paid any attention to the emotional life that had erupted into the discourse. Emotions are not considered relevant within these dominant modes of discourse today, all of which use only abstract concepts to communicate. In other words, although the participants' emotions were easily "visible" to the eyes of this shadow worker, they remained firmly "in the shadow" or psychic background of the debate. At no point were the emotions brought into consideration, as (psychic) factors whose neglect may contribute to the outcome of hardening positions and increasing polarization, to the point of splitting, in the debate.

When ignored emotional life is perceived with the eyes of the shadow worker, the impotent perplexity in the media, when dealing with one Donald Trump, starts to make sense. As I said earlier, the dominant modes of discourse [political, military (war-mongering), ideological, and economic] force commentators to squeeze Trump's "mad" rhetoric into narratives that rely exclusively on abstract language structures.

Attempts to "make sense" of Trump's speech in terms of given established policy formulations sound increasingly tortured. There is a psychic phenomenon in the background that, as yet, cannot be seen from within dominant cultural practices (economics, military, political). These practices *can* only see "things" (i.e., abstractions) a certain way, i.e. *literally* in terms of policies, etc. A fresh viewpoint is needed—that of the shadow worker, in order to discern this background.

I recently had this dream:

> A huge, whirlwind storm is emerging into visibility from (as?) a mountain and approaching us. Its self-originating light is partially obscured by a circus that is in the foreground—i.e., the artificial lights of the circus obscure it. Yet the storm itself *is* becoming visible.

After the dream I immediately thought of the Trump circus which, at this time, has gripped the American imagination. The establishment (or institutional mind) understands this eruption in terms of the three dominant cultural practices that can only see things one way i.e., as complete abstractions. To give you a further sense of how these practices perceive things today, I can refer back to the debate on Iran. One professor, speaking to the motion that the nuclear deal does not make the world a safer place, became exceptionally strident, shouting that her opponents just don't see things the right way. She said, "don't you see? If we make a deal with Iran, it will build a bomb anyway *and that's the reality* (her italics, i.e. practically screaming)!" Within her cultural practice of making foreign policy, a *possible* scenario of the unknown future *becomes* reality. The crucial distinction between imagining a future and present reality has collapsed.

And so it is with the Trump circus. We are all sensing an imminent *other* approaching us, in the background, or better, *as* the psychic background giving shape to current appearances, but we focus only on the visible foreground (the circus), which simply cannot be understood in terms of current dominant practices or modes of discourse. "Trump" therefore appears as a circus (everything turned upside down, wonky-wobble).

Our "official narratives" cannot give us the eyes to perceive the surface content (the circus) as transparent to an unknown *other*, an intelligence (the self-originating light) that is moving towards us in the form of mountain-vortex. Only the eyes of the shadow worker can give us this particular insight. We can get a glimpse of the proximity of the chaos through the shifting narrative in the mass media. For example in the movie, The Dark Knight (2008), the Joker says:

> Do I really look like a guy with a plan? You know what I am? I'm a dog chasing cars. I wouldn't know what to do with one if I caught it. You know, I just … do things. The mob has plans, the cops have plans, Gordon's got plans. You know, they're schemers,

schemers trying to control their little worlds. I'm not a schemer. I try to show the schemers how pathetic their attempts to control things really are. ... I just did what I do best. ... Introduce a little anarchy. Upset the established order, and everything becomes chaos. I'm an agent of chaos. Oh, and you know the thing about chaos? It's fair![25]

In a landmark debate between Charles Krauthammer and Bill O'Reilly, O'Reilly inadvertently reveals his inner convictions, and why, therefore, he supports Donald Trump, beggaring Krauthammer's belief, since he would surely eviscerate any other human being who dared to come on his show to make the kind of outlandish claims that Trump trumpets on a daily basis. Let's listen with an ear to the hidden depths of the relevant dialogue.

CK: Do you approve of [what Trump is doing]?

BO': I think what Donald Trump is doing is both good and bad. In the sense that he is destroying a corrupt system, it's good, and it's bad in the sense that he goes overboard, that he goes too far but our system is corrupt and people know it and he is destroying it.

CK: And the cure for corruption is to say things that you are admitting he doesn't really mean? You think that's the way you go after a corrupt system? ...

BO': It's corrupt, Charles, the whole damn system is corrupt, and Trump is blowing it up.

CK: I think it ought to be called for what it is— demagoguery. It's rather surprising that you would think that it is perfectly okay.

BO': I don't say that's perfectly okay ... I say that it is brilliant strategy. I say there is some worthiness to exposing a corrupt system. He is shaking everything up and maybe something good will come out of it because we can't keep going the way we're going. We can't! This country is in desperate trouble.[26]

O'Reilly is telling us, in words not so far removed from those of the Joker, that he also believes that any attempts to control things are "pathetic" and that chaos is the answer—"who knows, maybe something good will come of it."

Although we cannot yet know how this *other* will ultimately inform a new set of appearances as the real world, we can discern some hints from the image itself. I have received many "vortex" dreams and visions over a period of about thirty years now. I explore this symbol in some detail in my books.[27]

This dream shows that the psyche is bringing together both mountain and whirlwind. They belong together in some way.[28] With the help of my dream I must now learn to think turbulence and still point as belonging together in this one image. Of course if we think naturalistically, we know that the physical centre of a hurricane or vortex is a still point, but here we must ask the psychological question: in what way can turbulence *be* a still point, and *vice versa*?

Emotions, or emotional life, are felt to be a turbulent disturbance of calm abstract reasoning. The life of the emotions distracts us from the heights of abstract thinking and threatens its corresponding cultural forms (institutions of every kind). To allow emotional states into the debate as content or topics or focus of conscious attention, is to invite madness or chaos.

Yet this is exactly what Trump is doing! His form of discourse is "aimed at" stirring emotions, and nothing else![29] Reason, analysis, policy statements, sober appraisals of real-world conditions, are not relevant to this mode of discourse. This "circus" mode of discourse is felt only as frightening turbulence by the "establishment" which has, for so long, banished emotional *life* from all "official narratives". The only "still point" that our dominant cultural practices can perceive lies beyond all emotionality, beyond all sensual life, in a domain of sheer abstractions. So new thinking, from out of the unknown future, showing the "still point" *as* the very turbulence or emotionality that our culture eschews, can only mean, to the establishment, that a catastrophe is upon us.

While reactive forces gain momentum and resistance to this new thinking intensifies, the shadow worker can welcome this development emerging from the depths of Being, with love and an open, inquiring heart. We must indeed also acknowledge the imminence of catastrophe. Some cherished cultural forms, perhaps all, will be swept away. Perhaps the devastation will be greater than this, as many fear, speaking of a sixth mass extinction. This, too, must be faced as another imagination of the unknown future. I have had many such visions of this magnitude of disaster. Yet, even within these dire presentations, further mystery lies.

Turbulence, emotional life, chaos, *as* the new still point! How can this be? Emotional life is *life*! Our cultural practices and corresponding cultural forms have given us a way of existing that has increasingly excluded *life*. Over centuries of hardening thought, our language forms became increasingly representational (products of reflection, development of "world views", etc.) Then, a double catastrophe! We eventually forgot the *representational* nature of language and thus the "things" that such highly abstract language enable us to perceive (abstractions) became "seen" as being literally so—a historical process of increasing reification.[30] The turbulence of life is finally excluded altogether from our dominant modes of discourse and their correlative appearances.

It seems to me that a path to the wisdom of turbulence (emotional life) *as stillness* must involve an initiation into a new constitution of consciousness-reality. The initiate will perceive movement itself as the stable or still point. How can we do this without reifying "movement" into merely a new kind of "thing" that the old reality privileges? New psychological capacities will come into play here, leading to new cultural practices and correlative appearances in the real world. I present an example of such a practice in my book, Oblivion of Being. I can say here that such capacities must initially involve overcoming the privileged position of the subjective self (as author of all meaning) in favour of a new locus of subjectivity "in the phenomenon".

So, it will no longer be "what do I want" but rather, "how may I serve"?

VIRTUAL AND PHYSICAL REALITY

The collapse of the disjunction between fictional reality and empirical reality is now shown clearly with the invention of virtual reality which is a kind of positivized empirical reality. Virtual reality and empirical reality are beginning to interpenetrate in the most confounding and chaotic way, and as this essays shows, contemporary art is leading the way in exploring this weird phenomenon. I focus on one artwork, The Annunciation of the Virgin Deal by Grayson Perry, and once again, within this cultural product, I perceived seeds of possible new contours of the world, along with new cultural practices.

Heidegger made the fundamental discovery of a "world" that could also be called "the style of a culture". It is normally invisible and silent, "behind" our reflections on life and yet it determines just about everything to do with the way we live and understand how we live. The style of a culture or its "world" is "[l]ike the illumination in the room, [it] normally functions best to let us see things when we don't see it."[31]

In Heidegger's essay, The Origin of the Work of Art, he famously refers to van Gogh's painting, A Pair of Shoes. Starting with the shoes in their nature as equipment, he reveals a world that is so pervasive, surrounding the peasant woman at all points, that for her, it remains invisible. She simply wears her shoes, without noticing or reflecting on their nature as equipment. But, because they are presented to Heidegger as art, he *can* begin to describe the existential world that informs and shapes the life of the imagined peasant:[32] [33]

From out of the dark opening of the well-worn insides of the shoes the toil of the worker's tread stares forth. In the crudely solid heaviness of the shoes accumulates the tenacity of the slow trudge through the far-stretching and ever-uniform furrows of the field swept by a raw wind. On the leather lies the dampness and richness of the soil. Under the soles slides the loneliness of the field-path as evening falls. The shoes vibrate with the silent call of the earth, its silent gift of the ripening grain, its unexplained self-refusal in the wintry field. This equipment is pervaded by uncomplaining worry as to the certainty of bread, wordless joy at having once more withstood want, trembling before the impending birth, and shivering at the surrounding menace of death.

This vivid interpretation highlights Heidegger's understanding of the *function* of art to make manifest and articulate a world that is normally invisible and silent to those living in it, although remaining determined by it, in the routine, unreflective, daily use of the equipment (e.g. the peasant's shoes) that appears in the first place only by virtue of this world. It is this world, brought to language by Heidegger's existential phenomenology, that the peasant woman really lives in and is determined by, in all her conduct and style of living.

So, what world do *we* really live in, in 2016? I recently visited the Sydney 2016 Biennale: The theme of this art exhibition is the question:

[I]f each era has a different view of reality, what is ours? With our growing dependence on the virtual world of the Internet, the distinction between that world and the physical one is becoming ever less defined. Many artists are attempting to access the 'in-between'—the place where the virtual and the physical fold into one another. [34]

As I entered the first floor to buy my ticket, I glanced over to the souvenir shop and saw a reproduction of a work of art by one of the Biennale presenters, Grayson Perry.[35] I must have been ready or primed to receive this painting in a particular way, because in an illuminating moment, I shared Heidegger's understanding of art as manifesting and articulating the ordinarily hidden world that gives rise to all the appearances that we simply accept unreflectingly as "things" or "equipment", to be perceived or used by us in a meaningful and intelligent way. I am not able to reproduce Perry's artwork here but you can find an image on the Internet easily enough.[36]

Imagine a scene inside a modern home, filled with its quite ordinary things in their appearance as equipment. In the center is an angel—the angel of the Annunciation! I was immediately struck by the array of modern ordinary equipment taken for granted and used by the occupants of this house, on a daily basis. The angel and the Annunciation, the central figures in the painting, are not equipmental at all, and therefore perhaps not even an appearance in this (so far undisclosed) modern world. No one notices or pays any attention to her. Since the angel is not a manifest appearance (thing) in the world i.e., to the inhabitants, it seems likely that she is the artist's representation or personification of the world itself, *its self-disclosure*, to us, gazing at the artwork.

But let's start with the equipment!

We can see all the ordinary items that we use intelligently to move about in the dominant style of living of our modern culture—cups, coffee maker, magazine, cushions, tea towels, technological devices, etc. If we look more closely at these items, another feature that we normally take completely for granted begins to stand out—the ubiquitous presence of labels — "bourgeois and proud", "organic", "local", "plastic", "Penguin Books" (on the mugs); "make tea, not war" (on the towel), etc. The angel's body is portrayed as a cardboard cutout figure. She is pointing to portraits of Bill Gates and Steve Jobs that are hung on the wall. The iPad on the table is showing a news item, "Bakewell sells to Virgin for $270M."

Labels or advertising messages saturate our minds throughout our days and nights. We hardly notice them any more but they are the angels of our times (angel = messenger, as in the angel of the Annunciation, the title of the artwork). What are they announcing to us, through the artwork, as the self-disclosure of our world, or the style of our modern culture? Our senses are drawn to these labels involuntarily and we begin to think the message of the label unconsciously. Of course the advertising industry knows how to exploit our involuntary attention to its own advantage, giving every effort to ensure we reach for a particular product over the competition.

In thinking the thought of any label that pushes onto us, we human beings begin to think thoughts that are *alien* to any personal *empirical* experiences we might have. These alien thoughts bear a message from the concealed world that supports all these weird modern appearances. If you listen to interviews of the "man in the street", asking for his political opinions for example, you hear only the thought of the mass media at work. After all, how could most people have any *personal* experience of the horrors of terrorism, or the devastation of tropical rainforests, etc.? Yet this alien thought (i.e., alien to the personal empirical lives of most of us) is now determining the course of events in the empirical or physical world. The alien thought we unconsciously think by a kind of inductive process, belongs to another reality altogether—call it medial reality or virtual reality.

Virtual reality became possible *as a concept* when we began thinking reality exclusively in terms of the empirical senses i.e., the belief that everything we know about our reality comes from our senses. We call this reality empirical or physical reality. It is then only a small technical step to excite the senses directly with technologically generated information and call our subsequent experience "virtual reality" i.e. a reality is generated that is as close as possible in essence to physical reality. The *reality* aspect to virtual reality reminds us that we are immersed in a *real* world (of alien thought—thinking that is induced in us via excitation of the senses. Importantly, we interpret this thought as kind of solid substance, like the appearances of physical reality.[37]

At the same time we are physically surrounded by another real world—a world that determines the appearances that we use routinely on a daily basis: cups, towels, computers etc.[38]

Perry's artwork, then, is showing us an emerging new

world. Two worlds, virtual and physical are chaotically colliding, conflating, interpenetrating, uniting, fusing, but how do we *say* the possible world that may be emerging from this linguistic chaos? Take one piece of equipment, a cup. The label on the cup in Perry's artwork is an ad for a Penguin book. We are meant to think "Penguin Books" every time we lift up the cup to drink. What is the *mode of being* of such a piece of equipment?

We are meant to use the cup in its ordinary status as physical equipment to satisfy thirst, enjoy companionship with another, sooth anxieties, kill time etc., and at the same time, we are meant to think "Penguin Books", a thinking completely alien to the common equipmental status of a physical cup. Perry shows this concatenation of disjunctive thinking throughout his painting and in so doing is disclosing a world to us—one that is normally concealed from us, in order for the appearances to "shine forth" *as such* e.g. as an ordinary cup bearing a label.[39]

The cardboard angel of the Annunciation of the Virgin (the title of the work) is placed alongside an IPad announcing a sale to Virgin airlines, and she points to portraits of Bill Gates and Steve Jobs. Just underneath these portraits sits an ordinary mother and child—a new birth from out of our technological civilization? Is the angel announcing the birth of a new world, with *its* correlative appearances, cultural style, and practices? In Perry's painting, virtual reality is chaotically showing up *empirically*. Virtual reality and empirical reality are no longer to be thought as separate domains of "reality", in the way that fiction and science were once thought as quite separate domains of reality.

In one of my books, I describe an astounding video I found on YouTube.[40] The scene opens up with:

> Somewhere in a little town of Belgium
> On a square where nothing really happens
> We placed a button
> And waited for someone to push it …[41]

In the centre of the small town square is a pillar supporting a big red button. Dangling overhead is a sign: "Push to Add Drama". A passer-by does so and a drama erupts! Ambulances, accident victims, collisions between cars and people, fights, police and gangster shoot-outs all vie with one another while the local people look on. Although it is easy to get absorbed in the dramatic action, it is quite instructive to also cast an eye on the locals who watched this advertisement for a TV news station (as it turned out to be). Some were clearly shocked and then frightened. Others were nonplussed, uncertain, while still others became, in effect, the audience, enjoying the drama that exploded so unexpectedly into their lives "where nothing really happens".

A purely staged media event erupts into the empirical lives of ordinary people going about their business. It is striking to see how quickly some, if not most, understood what was happening and accepted it, even enjoying the "thrill" of it. This relatively quick adaptation to the incursion of drama into empirical life is reminiscent of earlier days when audiences at first fled the theatre as a cinematic train "rushed" towards them. Today we easily accept 3-D versions of these moving images, without thinking about the reality question at all. We merely enjoy the "thrill of the ride".

This staged event in which virtual reality (or medial reality) conflates with empirical (or physical) reality is merely another, more spectacular, example of the kind of appearances that Perry is drawing our attention to, in his painting. You can see this conflation everywhere in our daily lives. One more example will suffice. Here in Sydney, Rugby League is very important. Watching a game on TV is like watching two hours of computer pop-ups. Labels literally cover the bodies of the athletes; computer-generated and painted ads cover the playing field; digitalized ads run incessantly around the fence bordering the game. And it is all accepted now. These are the new appearances. Grayson Perry's artwork is an attempt by an artist to show us what world is being disclosed by these new appearances.

We can now return to the Sydney Biennale and the statement made by Stephanie Rosenthal:

> With our growing dependence on the virtual world of the Internet, the distinction between that world and the physical one is becoming ever less defined. Many artists are attempting to access the 'in-between'—the place where the virtual and the physical fold into one another.

The "place" where the virtual and physical "fold into one another" is a poetic way of pointing to the concealed (implicit) world that is "producing" these strange appearances (occurrents, equipment, as Heidegger would say) that we now take for granted. We are being shaped by this silent world as surely as van Gogh's peasant was shaped by the world that gave rise to her mode of being and *its* equipment (the boots). Perry's The Annunciation of the Virgin is one artist's way of disclosing this world, and we can see in his painting that this new world is passing strange indeed.

Throughout the last few decades, one of the major themes of my books concerns the actual process of manifestation of worlds. For example, in my book, Manifesting Possible Futures, I describe four conditions for the disclosure of worlds:

1. The individual effort of participation with an aspect of *possible* futures (the artist's imagination);

2. The enactment, by this individual, of his or her participation, thereby becoming a *mouthpiece* of this future (the artwork);

3. The willingness on the part of others to make a move towards conceiving the world the same way the individual does (emerging shared language);

4. The gradual congealing of that conception into the way the world is perceived, the world thus becoming, over time, "that way", resulting in cultural forms that give expression to and strengthen that new reality.

When these conditions are met then we, as psychological beings, and the real world in which we live, transform. We end up living in that world, accepting the new appearances and getting shaped by them. It becomes really so!

These four conditions are succinctly outlined and examined in the following passage by Owen Barfield

Imagination is not, as some poets have thought, simply synonymous with good. It may be either good or evil. As long as art remained primarily mimetic, the evil which imagination could do was limited by nature

… [b]ut … when the fact of the directionally creator relation is beginning to break through into consciousness, both the good and evil latent in the working of imagination begin to appear unlimited…. we could very well move forward into a chaotically empty or fantastically hideous world. …[42]:

One last point! It does seem to me at this time that we are collectively moving towards the "chaotically empty or fantastically hideous" world of appearances that Barfield warns us about. But this is only one possible future for us. Much hangs on how we understand "virtual reality" or more generally "technology".

Can we avoid the truth that our technological civilization produces a set of appearances that has come about through the physicalizing of (positivized) pure thinking? A simple transistor, for example is the materialization of a mathematical process of integration of equations. In other words, we have positivized what is in truth *negative* reality, thereby giving us a way to create our technological civilization—a civilization of "materialized (positivized) thought"—the world Grayson Perry is disclosing to us.[43]

Another possible future may emerge if we understand virtual reality as a positivized manifestation of a negative reality—what I would call the living "objective" psyche.[44] With this understanding we may become attuned to those appearances made possible by an interpenetration of the negatively real psyche *and* empirical reality—an interpenetration that some contemporary art is hinting at.

My recent essays and my books are asking the

question, what is the *speech* of this interpenetration, or this new birth—speech in Heidegger's sense that the essence of language is poesis, a disclosing of new world that "shines" *through* the new appearances?[45]

We must, I believe, look to living language as the originating inception of such new appearances and new cultural practices.

THE EXCEPTIONAL AND THE NORMAL

This essay was a contribution to the One Apple Film Festival held in Gosford, NSW in 2015. The Film Festival was part of the annual "Mental Health: Art Works!" exhibition. MHAW's mission is to showcase the effectiveness of the arts in mental illness and extreme states of mind. The Festival and this essay was inspired by a quote by Dr. Daniel Dorman: "If even one apple fell up, wouldn't we at least have to begin to question the laws of physics?" The quote comes from the documentary, Beyond The Medical Model, which presents the stories of "the exceptional" in the field of mental health.

Physics, or more generally, science, backed as it is by statistical analysis, privileges the commonplace (the normal, average, or expected), at the expense of the extraordinary (the outlier, the anomaly, the exception). General principles are privileged over particular instances. This approach has the advantage of providing us with a shared, stable perspective, as well as the power to predict the future. With a shared, stable perspective, or understanding, of reality, we gain certainty and security. Our entire Western civilization is constructed, through its manifold cultural practices, on this twin epistemological and psychological foundation of certainty and security. This foundation is evident also in the humanities, as we can see from this quote, from Edgar Wind, concerning our theories of history:

> There are historians, many of them admirable, who stress the importance of the commonplace in history. Their work is salutary and indispensable, because the commonplace is a relentless force. But insofar as their method is specially contrived to examine that particular subject, it is not suited to deal with the exceptional in history, the power of which should also perhaps not be underrated.[46]

The exceptional case, or the anomaly, can and indeed must be ignored, if we are to stabilize our understanding of reality and build coherent cultural practices that, in effect, tell us who we are. The other typical way to deal with annoying anomalies is to assimilate them to the governing knowledge systems.

We do this by inventing a new category when necessary so that the anomaly can be understood in terms of available knowledge and then "treated" in a way as to restore familiar certainty and security. I'll give one example from the "voice hearers" culture. The category of "voice hearer" was invented as an alternative to that of "psychosis" or "schizophrenia". Once that new category was formed, many people could thus find a viable place in the *given* culture. They became more acceptable to the otherwise frightened community. The same occurs with the labels of "alcoholic" and "addict". Once the category is in place, cases "magically" appear (look at ADD, autism, too!) and we can get to know them in the way that science knows today. Certainty and security are re-established for all (even if some suffer the effects of being known in the way that science knows i.e., known as an object of investigation.

This common and now standardized approach to mental illness does, as I said, assure certainty and security in the culture. Even if individuals fall between categories, that does not lead to uncertainty and insecurity in the system, as a rule. The system invents a "catch-all" category for such anomalies, atypical depression or schizotypal personality disorder being pertinent examples.

There is one exception to this "rule". What happens if the anomalies begin to accumulate to the point where they can no longer be ignored, or assimilated, and they begin to intrude inconveniently into the established body of cultural practices that together tell us who we are and what is real?

We are in such a time now. So there is one way I disagree with Dr. Dorman. If only one apple falls up, our culture does not willingly interpret that wayward apple as a challenge to our entire cultural perspective on reality. Not by any means! Our institutions go on quite happily, ignoring the anomaly; or if there is some momentary discomfort caused by the inconvenience of a single apple, we alternatively simply invent a way for the wayward apple to appear to be going down all along, even if in a deviant fashion. Think of some of the historical attitudes towards homosexuality for example. Individuals were interpreted as "wanting" to be normal like the rest but as lacking the moral fibre, or gene, religious guidance, or whatever, to do so—they were interpreted as awkwardly-falling-down-type apples! Look at all the sub-categories within schizophrenia for example—so much actual uncertainty, masked by the authority of categories and subcategories.

But, as I have suggested, annoying anomalies are accumulating today; too many apples are falling up, too many to ignore, too many to categorize and pathologize. What happens next is a bit frightening! A crack appears. Our stable perspective on reality is called into question. The way things appear to us, that define us, is no longer quite so stable as it has been, for centuries. We are used to the "facts of life" being stable, known with certainty. We are used to feeling secure in that knowledge of the facts. But what if the accumulation of anomalies, or "exceptional cases", is demonstrating to us that the facts themselves are changing?

Impossible! How do facts change? After all, a fact is "what is known to be true"!

It has happened before. In previous times, for example, the moon was known to be the gateway to the soul-world or the home of the dead. It's no good saying that our ancestors merely believed such things and were mistaken as to the truth. Entire cultures developed meaningful cultural practices that expressed such truths, and therefore people *lived* in accord with those truths, just like we do today with our truths. Truths, facts do undergo transformation at times— and those times of transformation are also the times of privileging the exceptional!

As Edgar Wind further says, in relation to historical research:

> It seems to be a lesson of history that the commonplace may be understood as a reduction of the exceptional, but that the exceptional cannot be understood by amplifying the commonplace. Both logically and causally the exceptional is crucial, because it introduces (however strange it may sound) the more comprehensive category.[47]

I take this to mean that our efforts to assimilate extreme states of consciousness, for example, into known categories that belong to the commonplace is like the part trying to understand the whole. Our stable perspective on reality is getting challenged by a plethora of extreme states of mind that are harbingers of an emerging perspective on reality that is yet to be formed and made stable by a *new* set of cultural practices. We are between stable perspectives at present and everything is therefore uncertain and insecure.

Chaos!

Are there any coherent cultural practices that can both support us in this time of uncertainty and insecurity and help those who are in an extreme state of consciousness? As we can see in this festival, there are any number of alternative and standardized approaches to "the exceptional," or as we might say, extreme forms of consciousness. In my view, efforts that go towards inventing new categories, even if the aim is to be less judgmental, more inclusive, more democratic, must be seen in terms of supporting the preferred downward motion of all apples, i.e. supporting the perspective on reality that has built up over centuries through the scientific way of knowing: i.e. knowing *things*.

Any person in an extreme state of mind can be made into an *object* of scientific inquiry once a category has been invented for her or him. This move supports current reality—a reality that is now developing serious cracks as "the exceptional" continues to challenge its *truth*, its facts.

While some, perhaps many, professionals today undertake the task of maintaining our present perspective on knowledge and the truth of our current reality, there needs to be room for those who take on the task of what may be called "preparing the future".

It seems that such individuals are drawn from the ranks, so to speak, of those who undergo an extreme state of mind, spiritual emergency, kundalini-type experience, "shamanic initiation", etc., They are "given" this task of preparing the future not by any external authority and certainly not by any *available* cultural practice. They are given their task by the experience itself.

With this understanding of at least some forms of spiritual emergency, we can begin to see that preparing the future, as a task, involves three major aspects. The first is to articulate the emerging new perspective of reality; the second is to work towards new forms of cultural practices that can bring the new perspective into actuality and stabilize it; the third is to accompany other people going through similar extreme, initiatory, and culture-changing experiences. These three aspects, taken together, are what I mean by "preparing the future."

At this time, can anything be said at all about the new perspective of reality that is intruding so inconveniently into our current one? I think something can be said about its essential quality. This quality seems to be shared among all the varieties of spiritual emergency, extreme states of mind, psychoses, some UFO experiences, hearing voices, etc. Although it can be easily articulated, we must also be mindful that those going through the experience can be shattered by its intensity. It does indeed involve an upturning of reality itself!

The details of what I am about to say are far too complex for one essay. I have worked for thirty years finding ways to articulate what I can say only in a few words here. My books and video talks are available for a more nuanced and detailed description but I can begin by noting that our present stable perspective on reality rests on an essential *disjunction* between what may be called empirical reality (given the status of truth by science and its epistemology) and fictional "reality", by which we mean all the *unverifiable* aspects of existence, given the status of untruth, or simply, fiction.

The anomalies or exceptional states of mind that are turning up today in bewildering numbers seem to share the following essential characteristic: The *disjunction* between empirical reality and fictional "reality" is getting destroyed and the question of which reality is the *real* reality is turning inside out! Individuals undergoing extreme states of mind are calling empirical reality a lie or an untruth, claiming instead that the *real* reality is "fictional" in some new strange new sense of "fictional". To make matters worse, these individuals are experiencing, like the proverbial canary in the coal mine, a breakdown in the disjunction between the two realities.

Fictional reality is turning out to have the same qualities as empirical reality once had, while the certainty and security of empirical reality dissolves. The logic of difference seems to be giving way to the logic of some form of interpenetration of empirical reality and fictional "reality" (although now not "reality" but *reality*).

This is about as confusing as it can get but is, I am convinced, the essence of what constitutes modern experiences of extreme states of mind, and its "aim" is to prepare the future, as I said above, as a new logic of interpenetration.

We could also put it this way: art (fictional reality) and life (empirical reality) are beginning to interpenetrate, causing (as in Aristotle's final cause i.e. a "cause" pulling us from the future) a breakdown in current reality—a *cultural* psychosis.

Once an individual's extreme state of mind can be seen *this* way, his or her ordeal starts to make a whole lot of sense and she or he can be helped to prepare the future by navigating his or her experience to its conclusion. We can see the UFO phenomenon, for example, where abductees will not surrender their conviction that the experimental surgery imposed on them by aliens is concretely real, even though there is no empirical evidence; or voice hearers who perceive voices or presences in a way indistinguishable from their ordinary senses; or those on a shamanic journey who are dismembered without the benefit of the psychological protection of an "as if."

We also may cast a wider eye to our culture, and find a number of cultural happenings that hint at this interpenetration of art and life.

For example, in the contemporary art scene, with forms such as installation art, or performance art where the artist *is* the art; or in the explosion of interest in new genres of literature where the reference of the text has become an ongoing problematic; or in biography where confabulation seems to be on equal epistemological footing as historical fact; or in the interrogation of the relation between literature and philosophy; or in depth psychology where strange concepts such as the *reality* of the objective psyche are being refined; or in physics with the mind-bending contradiction in the nature of light (both an immaterial wave and material particle).

I will conclude with this thought. Individuals undergoing an extreme state of mind, do indeed suffer, and suffer dreadfully, throughout. It is a natural response of the healer to want to relieve that suffering and return that person to a normal life, as far as possible. Many sufferers want only that too. We now have the technical capacity to direct our treatment to the causal body (the brain) and chemically to reduce or even remove that suffering by altering that causal body.

These predominant forms of treatment, when done exclusively, ensure that any *meaning* in the suffering remains occluded. There is a big difference between seeking meaning and seeking causes. I believe the deepest meaning in these forms of illness lies in the image of preparing the future, as I have outlined above.

The healer concerned with meaning must therefore be able to perceive hints of the unknown future appearing from within the "psychotic" content of the "initiate".

Speaking or reflecting these hints back to the individual undergoing the ordeal can assist in articulating the unknown future reality. The unknown future can then be further prepared by artistic means, which are often forced upon the initiate by the process itself. This dual healing process seems to stabilize the individual who may then gain confidence that his or her experience is not only a meaningless descent into madness (a prominent feature of any kind of breakdown), but also a meaningful breakthrough into a new way of being that may serve the interests of *both* individual and culture.

IS IT TOO LATE ... TO GET SMART?

In the popular comedy series, "Get Smart", the final credits show agent Maxwell Smart leaving the "Control Building" and striding purposefully towards the future. As he does so, three doors slam thunderously shut behind him. He pauses as if he has forgotten something. He turns and walks back only to have the fourth door close with equal finality on his nose. He cannot go back! It's too late! Too late?

Language or styles of language can become a door that opens up to the background movements of our cultural productions, *if* we can loosen the hold that the inner/outer disjunction has on our thinking and perceptions of phenomena. In this way we can get glimpses of both our current trajectory into the unknown future and also inceptive movements that may produce new language and new cultural practices.

You will see how I do this in this and my other essays. For example, in this essay, as I read the text of another author, a dream surfaced, and I immediately include it in my essay as a further hint of the unknown future.

For me, cultural phenomena can open up to those "background" movements that are shaping all our cultural productions in the first place. These background movements are most often unknown to the artist who considers only his or her conscious intentions (exceptions include the kind of art that "allows" accidents). By reading a movie, or art piece as a text, we can get hints of these background movements implicit in those texts, and thus give voice to them as a way of welcoming the unknown future. And so, the images or "text" of the "credits" scene in Get Smart became transparent to me and I gained a further hint of the trajectory we are taking in relation to the unknown future.

The memory of this scene suddenly broke into my recent musings on language, vocabulary, and modern cultural practices. I was trying to probe more deeply into a question that has held me for many years, assuming different forms, and leading me into fresh paths of inquiry. In its latest form, the question asks: what cultural practice could nudge us off our present course towards unmitigated disaster and, at the same time, reflect and support a narrow possible, real, and desirable path towards another future?

Descriptions of our present trajectory towards catastrophe are readily drawn from almost any discipline today, as reported in the mass media. But all these *descriptions* have something in common—a privileged style of language along with its correlative, dominant cultural practices, which I will explore a little later. This style of language can be thought of as a pragmatic language, simply a tool for use by us, no longer carrying any metaphysical pretensions.

Accordingly, all notions of mind, consciousness, truth, experience, the eternal, etc. are now *naturalized*, i.e. thought of in the same way that evolutionary biology and empirical psychology are both now thought, i.e. as completely contingent. Language, as Richard Rorty says, is now commonly regarded as a toolbox, holding different tools for different tasks, in accordance with our beliefs and desires, to help us reach our purposes or goals.[48] The structure of language is now no different from that of brains, computers, or galaxies—it carries no privileged "metaphysical" importance, or meaning.

For example, this passage is taken at random following a quick search of the Internet:

> Green politics (also known as Eco-Politics) is a political ideology that aims to create an ecologically sustainable society rooted in environmentalism, nonviolence, social justice, and grassroots democracy.[49]

We know what is being said here. All these words are embedded in a network of vocabularies and practices or styles of living and we all use such language instrumentally and intelligently, as this author does. As Rorty says, there is no need to look "behind" these words to find an invisible "eternal" meaning. Their "meaning" lies in how we use them. This sentence, once read, could easily lead us into intelligent, relevant, political or social action whose purpose would be clear —e.g. to do something effective about our dangerous trajectory towards ecological disaster. We have no need to focus on the words or sentences as such. We simply use them to our own ends. This instrumental view of language is dominant today in the modern world and its corresponding cultural practices are ones of dominance and control—how can I achieve the aims I want (desire) according to what I believe to be desirable? Rorty goes on to describe this dominant and prevailing view of language:

> Consider sentences as strings of marks and noises emitted by organisms, strings capable of being paired off with the strings we ourselves utter (in the way we call "translating"). Consider beliefs, desires, and intentions — sentential attitudes generally — as entities posited to help predict the behavior of these organisms. Now think of those organisms as gradually evolving as a result of producing longer and more complicated strings, strings which enable them to do things they had been unable to do with the aid of shorter and simpler strings. Now think of us as examples of such highly evolved organisms, of our highest hopes and deepest fears as made possible by, among other things, our ability to produce the peculiar strings we do ...[50]

In the same passage, Rorty makes it clear that he is not privileging this view of language. In his typically democratic fashion, he is simply saying that this prevailing view is one of an infinite number of possible views. This particular one prevails simply because it has its advantageous uses for us. It just so happens that understanding language (and minds, or consciousness, etc.) in the same way that we currently understand objects in the world has its distinct advantages. As he puts it, "not until Freud did we get a usable way of thinking of ourselves as machines to be tinkered with, a self-image that enabled us to weave terms describing psychic mechanisms into our strategies of character-formation."[51]

Rorty is not imposing his own ideology on us here. He is eloquently saying what is happening in our current cultural practices and I do not think he can be doubted on this point. Most, if not all, cultural practices today are rooted in language that helps us characterize nature and ourselves as mechanical parts of a greater machine:

> Whereas everybody from Plato to Kant had identified our central self, our conscience, the standard-setting, authoritative part of us, with universal truths, general principles, and a common human nature, Freud made conscience just one more, not particularly central, part of a larger, homogenous machine. He identified the sense of duty with the internalization of a host of idiosyncratic, accidental episodes.

> On his account our sense of moral obligation is not a matter of general ideas contemplated by the intellect, but rather of traces of encounters between particular people and our bodily organs. He saw the voice of conscience not as the voice of the part of the psyche that deals with generalities as opposed to the part that deals with particulars, but rather as the (usually distorted) memory of certain very particular events.[52]

The main characteristic of a machine, of course, is that the parts are related only mechanically, infinitely replaceable, with no "mystery" or spiritual being that can unite the parts in any way other than by simple numerical addition. The parts are not "held together" by a secret spiritual unity. As we can see in the quote above—accidents, idiosyncrasies, memories as traces of a literal past, conscience as internalized real past events —this is a world of contingency only and Rorty describes it very well, without prejudice, I think. He is telling us pretty much how it is with us today, in our cultural practices. Where there are gaps in our vocabularies, there is no need to insert God, or mystery, a psyche, or the unknown abyss, etc.:

> The trouble with making a big deal out of language, meaning, intentionality, the play of signifiers, or *differance* is that one risks losing the advantages gained from appropriating Darwin, Nietzsche, and Dewey. Once one starts reifying language, one begins to see gaps opening between the sorts of things Newton and Darwin describe and the sorts Freud and Derrida describe, instead of seeing convenient divisions within a toolbox - divisions between batches of linguistic tools useful for various different tasks. One begins to be enthralled by phrases like "the unconscious is structured like a language," because one begins to think that languages must have a distinctive structure, utterly different from that of brains or computers or galaxies (instead of just agreeing that some of the terms we use to describe language might, indeed, usefully describe other things, such as the unconscious). [53]

For example, a conundrum within neuroscience, at least for some, is how do we "get" across a linguistic gap from a vocabulary of physical science to a vocabulary of mind (i.e. the gap between mind and body). For the now dominant cultural practices of our time, there is simply no need to unite these vocabularies. They are as Rorty says useful each in its own way—different tools within the language toolbox!

For Rorty and Pragmatism, it is very democratic to be de-centred in this way. No vocabulary should hold sway over any other. No belief system should drown out any other. There is room for all perspectives and there is no need to generate a central one that unifies or dominates any other. Everything leveled! As a Neo-Pragmatist, Rorty is not saying that democracy is the only way to go. He openly declares that it is the cultural practice that he simply prefers, based on his beliefs and desires:

> My theme, however, is different. I want to focus on the way in which Freud, by helping us see ourselves as centerless, as random assemblages of contingent and idiosyncratic needs rather than as more or less adequate exemplifications of a common human essence, opened up new possibilities for the aesthetic life. He helped us become increasingly ironic, playful, free, and inventive in our choice of self-descriptions.[54]

So far, I have inserted some quotes from American Pragmatism, and shared the views of a eloquent spokesman of our times, Richard Rorty, in order to bring home, as un-prejudicially as possible, where we are going as we continue to valorize this democratic vocabulary and its various cultural practices, rooted as it is in a view of everything, yes, everything, as a sum of mechanical parts which are forever replaceable, able to be utilized for this or that purpose at will, and expendable when no longer needed.

All Rorty is doing is bringing this description of nature and ourselves home to us. He understands that those who quail, or shrink from this view of life, must be holding on to another, usually metaphysical view, of ourselves or nature, a view that has had its day (for example, the view that we each are an essential self that is precious and irreplaceable, or that the various parts of the world are united through God or a central Meaning, or that there is a reality called the imagination through which the universal can appear within the particular, etc.)

I have personally experienced shockwaves over many years, as the "metaphysical" vocabulary I favored collided with our modern instrumental one. I needed a vocabulary of unity through the imagination, interpenetration of universals and particulars, essence and contingency, language as alive, psychic reality, *otherness* that contained me and spoke to me, and so on. I still do!

The shockwaves occurred as I tried to use that vocabulary in the modern world which most assuredly, as Rorty tells us, has moved on, no longer needing these terms to describe the world or the entities within it. It's another linguistic world now, and it has taken me decades to catch up to it in my personal life and my chosen cultural practice of depth psychology and therapy. I have noticed for example that people coming to see me have less and less interest in dreams, or interiority, or imagination. They simply want me to solve their problems. They are the modern ones and I am the passé one, in our styles of discourse.

Rorty raises this question of outdated vocabulary in relation to Heidegger when he asks if Heidegger has any (philosophical) right to feel the nostalgia that is evident in his later writing! He is suggesting that Heidegger has not caught up with himself and with what he knows to be true of our modern technological civilization.

It is at first a bitter, dare I say, *medicine* to drink from this cup. But I did. I did it by reading Richard Rorty (and others) as a mouthpiece of our modern democratic times, from cover to cover, several times, in a "true" (I hope) hermeneutic fashion—I felt my gorge rise from time to time, but re-read the offending passage again and again until I settled down and began to read the passage as "Rorty" might read it.

In other words, his text entered me and I began to speak it from the place where the man Rorty and the man Woodcock belong to the same time, the time of mechanization of everything. Then I realized that I in fact already had been thinking all along what he was thinking—two modern men born into this time when a particular perspective, let's call it the "decentered" world of assemblages of parts, has gained a global dominance over all other perspectives.

I could now examine this perspective on language, life, us, etc., without recoiling in horror, even as the cultural practices that have sprung up as expressions of this perspective are most assuredly leading us towards the cliff.

I now realize with conviction how telling that little "credits" scene from Get Smart is. Our modern perspective (we are all simply assemblages of replaceable parts) continues to take hold, and door after door closes behind us, as we march purposefully towards whatever personal future we choose, based on whatever desire and beliefs we may contingently have at the time of choosing. If we indulge in a nostalgic moment (as I surely have over the years—many such moments), and naively attempt to return to past and passé perspectives, then, like Maxwell Smart, we may find ourselves with a bruised nose, with another, final door slammed shut in our faces.

There is no turning back.

So, is there a path forward, as I asked earlier, a path that may steer us away from catastrophe, towards another possible, more viable future? It may surprise you to hear, after all this, that Richard Rorty describes such a way, without prescribing it, of course. Rorty's interpretation of Heidegger's project is, as we could expect, democratically tolerant. Let's begin this inquiry by entering Rorty's interpretation of language according to Heidegger:

> One way to describe what Heidegger does in his later work is to see him as defending the poets against the philosophers. More particularly, we should take him at his word when ... he says: "In the end, the business of philosophy is to preserve the force of the most elemental words ... and to keep the common understanding from levelling them off to that unintelligibility which functions as a source of pseudo-problems. ...
>
> When a word is used frequently and easily, when it is a familiar, ready-to-hand instrument for achieving our purpose, we can no longer hear it." Heidegger is saying that we need to be able to hear the "most elemental" words which we use ... rather than simply using these words as tools. We need to hear them in the way in which a poet hears them when deciding whether to put one of them at a certain place in a certain poem. By so hearing them we shall preserve what Heidegger calls their "force." We shall hear them

in the way in which we hear a metaphor for the first time.[55]

Let's slow down here to hear Rorty's interpretation of Heidegger. He is saying that there are two ways to hear words—one is the common, instrumental way of using language for this or that purpose. We know for example what that passage above, drawn from Green Politics, means in that we can easily link it to future intelligent action or research within that vocabulary. Rorty is saying however that there is another way to listen to language, one that is not utilitarian at all. It is the way of the poet, according to Heidegger:

> [H]e wants to direct our attention to the difference between inquiry and poetry, between struggling for power and accepting contingency. He wants to suggest what a culture might be like in which poetry rather than philosophy-cum-science was the paradigmatic human activity. [56]

Rorty (through Heidegger) is suggesting an entirely different view of language and an entirely different cultural practice. The time to consider this *poetic* perspective on language is, according to Rorty:

> when things are not going well, when a new generation is dissatisfied, when the young have come to look at what is being done in a given genre as hackwork, or as so overburdened with what Thomas Kuhn calls "anomalies" that a new start is needed. In such periods, people begin to toss around old words in new senses, to throw in the occasional neologism, and thus to hammer out a new idiom which initially attracts attention to itself and only later gets put to work.[57]

We surely are now in such a time!

The instrumental perspective on language cannot possibly allow us to feel the force of metaphor heard for the first time. Rorty rather astonishingly adds that "our culture has not only been carried upward by a bubbling fountain of puns and metaphors [which later become dead or literalized in the normal course of instrumentalizing language, as we put them to work—my insert]; it has been increasingly conscious of itself as resting on nothing more solid than such a geyser."[58]

I say, "astonishing", because when I read this passage, a dream I had in 1988 burst up from the depths, geyser-like. Sometimes you have to wait a long time to understand the speech of a particular dream. Here it is now, twenty-eight years later:

> The end of the world is nigh. Someone says that the US budget deficit is 1 trillion dollars. The nuclear bombs are upon us. I am to be imprisoned for 3 years with my son in a hut but I get up and walk out as no one is around. Now I am at the top of a ravine with water at the bottom. It looks terrifying. Others leap in and I finally do. The water is actually bubbling up keeping us buoyant and tremendous power in it.

Most of my subsequent work over the years, it now seems, is simply a re-statement or refinement of the speech of that dream. The character of my writing includes such moments of "geyser eruptions," right in the middle for my more sober reflections. I have learned to follow that flow and surrender my instrumentalist perspective of language in favor of a more "poetic" release of metaphoric language. In fact, this essay also has such moments included in it. What follows now is a sustained burst of geyser-like language that came upon me as I wrestled with Rorty's thought. It began with my returning to the title of my essay, Too Late to ... Get Smart?

Let me begin by asking a question of you, my reader. How did you read the title? Did you read it instrumentally, i.e. a means to get into the body of my essay—an obscure summation, perhaps? This is what we do in accordance with the dominant paradigm today which asserts that language, along with everything else is an instrument at our disposal, according to whatever beliefs and desires we have at the moment. Nothing wrong about that, of course! I am not here to instruct anyone on correct behavior. However, in the light of this being a troubled time, to put it very mildly—well, on second thoughts, why put it mildly? Let's put it the way my dream says it: "The end of the world is nigh. ... I am at the top of a ravine with water at the bottom. It looks terrifying ."

Under these dire circumstances we could practice slowing down long enough to hear words in the way Heidegger suggests, i.e., towards "the preparatory work of restoring force to the most elementary words." Words gain force when they are experienced as metaphors coming out of nowhere, lightning bolts which blaze new trails.[59] If we slow down enough to hear the words of my title another way, what might happen? I discovered to my astonishment that there is an ambiguity to be found.

"Get Smart" certainly can be construed instrumentally as an admonition for us to get smart, wake up, come to our senses, use our intelligence, before it is too late. But it also can be understood as an admonition to *understand* Smart. Can we understand Smart, i.e. Maxwell Smart the protagonist of my story here, before it is too late? This interpretation held some wonder for me. It was not explicit and yet held me in its grip. I decided to dig deeper. The word "smart" is meant several different ways that depend on the context. It can mean:

1. showing mental alertness and calculation and resourcefulness

2. painfully severe

3, characterized by quickness and ease in learning

4. elegant and stylish

5. quick and brisk

6. capable of independent and apparently intelligent action • smart weapons

7. improperly forward or bold

So far, this kind of etymological digging is good solid, utilitarian word work. But I felt something akin to Heidegger's force drawing me to only two of those dictionary meanings which therefore "stood out" for me. What could pain have to do with mental alertness, calculation, and resourcefulness (Items 1 and 2)? You see there is nothing predictable or even useful in pairing those two meanings but there was a compelling force to that pairing, even a shock-like effect. I could not ignore it. So, I am now plunging into that dream ravine …[60]

I am somehow to understand Smart, that modern protagonist embodying "mental alertness, calculation, and resourcefulness" in a way that is related to pain, even severe pain. Is Smart smarting? If Smart is a metaphor of the dominant perspective that views everything as machinery to be exploited for any purpose, is there pain *in* that perspective too. Or does that perspective *cause* pain somewhere? Is it painful to be seen that way, or to see others that way, i.e. as replaceable parts of a great machine? Can understanding Smart have something to do with understanding the pain that comes with privileging Smart's perspective, as we all do today?

Now all this is interesting because *machinery* doesn't feel anything! All our efforts today are in lockstep with the "machinery" perspective. We are building tremendous momentum towards becoming machines, backed by our united, unwavering conviction that we must, simply must, eliminate pain and suffering at all costs. The next quarry after that is death itself. We seek to conquer death by becoming more and more machine-like.

Yet, to understand Smart, this worldwide dominant cultural practice, with its utilitarian vocabulary of machinery, is now, for me, to understand the *pain* of its "mental alertness, calculation, and resourcefulness." How can such a way of being be painful when its practices, language, and styles of discourse are producing a world that is pain-free. It is easy and obvious to claim that the pain lies with organic life suffering the effects of being reduced to an exploitable resource in the service of enhancement and efficiency. But I am warned away from this obvious response. Something nudges me in another direction. I receive another image, a movie I once saw. "Look there," a quiet voice tells me.

The movie is called Dark City (1998). Briefly, the movie concerns a group of foreboding figures called "the Strangers" who are experimenting with human beings. We learn that they are in fact:

> endangered extraterrestrial parasites who use corpses as their hosts. Having a hive mind, the Strangers have been experimenting with humans to analyze their individuality in the hopes that some insight might be revealed that would help their race survive.[61]

The experiments are disastrous failures and human protagonist Murdoch eventually informs them that they are looking in the wrong place—the human mind—in order to understand human beings as individuals.

Now, as I sit here pondering the sudden intrusion of this movie, with its strange, disturbing plot, I try to bring to words what I am being shown from within this nexus of words and images, drawn from so many different sources. There is something here that hasn't been said before, that cannot simply be assimilated back into the familiar style of discourse that dominates today. How can a style of discourse at once be mentally alert, calculating, and resourceful *and* filled with pain, even as it seeks to make a world without pain, without suffering, without death? Is there a pain or suffering implicit in the cultural practices that spring from the dominant mechanical view of life—a view that paradoxically eschews pain altogether?

While we human beings each obviously understand personal suffering, at least to some degree, there is also *logic of suffering*. We can get closer to this logic (or way of thinking) through studying initiation rituals, all of which include some form of penetrating the body—ordeals, scarification, cuts, piercings, tooth removal, fingers cut off, head shaved, circumcision, etc. The logic of these methods was not one of stoic forbearance, willing self-sacrifice, punishment, discipline, or sadistic pleasure etc. It was to "install" an unwavering knowledge of what may be called the reigning power of Being. The initiate's subjectivity or personality was not in question. He or she simply was to submit humbly to penetration by *something else* that in fact determined his or her life but now, also, through the efficacy of the physical ordeal, ruled as the truth of the initiate's life. This penetration went to the core in the sense that the whole being of the initiate was engaged in participation with the process of penetration or "bringing home the message".

There was of course often intense suffering that accompanied such procedures (some lasting days) but the logic of *something else*, something determinative, fateful, decisively penetrating the initiate and bringing itself to consciousness within the initiate's mind is the logic of suffering. And with these profound processes, we can no longer say with certainty whose suffering it is. The logic of initiatory suffering is the logic of being penetrated by a greater *other* who wishes to enter one and come to consciousness "within" one, by participating with the consciousness or mind of the initiate.

In modern times we have been enthralled by the dominant perspective which seeks to eliminate suffering by viewing us, and everything else, as equal replaceable parts of a machine. We have been seduced by its power to shape a world according to its will—the very purpose that the Strangers accomplished in the movie, Dark City —and we have been eager to pursue a life style that promises satisfaction of every desire, given any contingent belief we may have.

But, we have not yet been *initiated* by this modern phenomenon as our *spiritus rector*!

Instrumental language has foreclosed (the first closed door) on any experience of this language as a conscious phenomenon with its own intelligence, having the character of a greater *other*—perhaps *the* greater *other* of our time—our modern version of the reigning power of Being! Like the Strangers in the movie who aimed at the wrong part of the human being to penetrate and know themselves, this perspective, as a phenomenon, is aiming to initiate us into *its* greater reality—and the appropriate target of that aim lies not in the mind but in the human heart, as Murdoch informs the Strangers.[62]

But instrumental language, which we greedily adopt and use for our own purposes, prevents any linguistic access to the heart, in any way other than the literal way —heart attacks, surgery, etc. (the second closed door). Finally, because we can now comfortably live in the world created by such vocabulary and cultural practices, there appears to be no incentive to be otherwise As Aldous Huxley's Brave New World anticipates (the third closed door):

> Spending time alone is considered abnormal and even reprehensible, and well-adjusted citizens spend their leisure in communal activities requiring no thought.

This leads to a lifestyle which readers may see as shallow and hedonistic. It is promoted by the ready availability and universally-endorsed consumption of the hallucinogenic drug *soma* (an allusion to a ritualistic drink of the same name consumed by ancient Indo-Aryans), and by the promotion of recreational sex, often as a group activity. [63]

The way through this time and its language of mechanization along with its relevant cultural practices, towards a different possible future, is of course a path of initiation. Suffering is the key, in its initiatory sense, i.e. our being penetrated to the core by the reality of our dominant perspective and its message. The human inhabitants of the movie Dark City endure the probing experiments of the Strangers who, for example, inserted different sets of memory each night so that their guinea pigs would wake up each day as different people. But only one man wakes up to the Strangers *as a real phenomenon* that was determining his and others' lives. Only he, therefore, *suffers* its penetrations into the core of his being, bringing with it a message of understanding—his destiny. Only he therefore could become a generator of a new world, one that in this case is based on Love. And he could only do so once he overcame himself, through the efficacy of the initiatory process.

This fourth door of initiation may be closed to us as well. The key to keeping it open lies in whether we can *experience* our dominant world perspective of instrumentalism, coupled with control and power, as a real phenomenon, with its own consciousness and intelligence—an "alien" *other* that seeks to penetrate us for its own purposes, leaving its message inscribed in our hearts—a scar, if you like, which, in logical terms is a memory prompt, or "sacred" text, not a disfigurement. I am well aware that the vocabulary I am using just now does not belong to any instrumental view of language. It is, instead, metaphor at work; the kind of "poetic" vocabulary that Rorty believes is necessary in a time "overburdened with what Thomas Kuhn calls 'anomalies'".

Is there any field or cultural practice where we can perceive such an overburden of anomalies already taking place? I think there is. In a previous paper I address the question of burgeoning anomalies in the field of mental health, in terms of a distinction between psychosis and spiritual emergency:

> Individuals undergoing an extreme state of mind, do indeed suffer, and suffer dreadfully, throughout. It is a natural response of the healer to want to relieve that suffering and return that person to a normal life, as far as possible. Many sufferers want only that too. We now have the technical capacity to direct our treatment to the causal body (the brain) and chemically to reduce or even remove that suffering by altering that causal body.

> These predominant forms of treatment, when done exclusively, ensure that any *meaning* in the suffering remains occluded. There is a big difference between seeking meaning and seeking causes. I believe the deepest meaning in these forms of illness lies in the image of preparing the future, as I have outlined above. The healer concerned with meaning must therefore be able to perceive hints of the unknown future appearing from within the "psychotic" content

of the "initiate". Speaking or reflecting these hints back to the individual undergoing the ordeal can assist in articulating the unknown future reality. The unknown future can then be prepared by artistic means, which are often forced upon the initiate by the process itself.[64]

There is a growing movement throughout the world that accepts this distinction, that perceives "spiritual emergency" where the medical profession only sees psychosis. Within this nascent cultural practice, "poetic" methods of addressing spiritual emergencies are privileged over pharmaceutical procedures that seek only to normalize the condition.[65] These new cultural practices can only have come into being with the discovery of a new vocabulary, a new perspective born from the experiences of some individuals, somewhere, who have, as Heidegger says, suffered the illuminating bolt of lightning, or the uprising geyser of metaphors.

Many of these individuals were prepared for this initiation through their own spiritual emergency, which really is simply saying they arrived at that psychological "place" where they began to experience our current modern perspective, as an alien *other*, a very real phenomenon, rather than simply a useful tool to exploit and use others and nature. Many such people have been treated as useful tools themselves and we commonly call the outcome of this practice, "trauma".

To be a victim of trauma is a major social issue today, and a major cultural practice. It can also constitute the fourth door remaining open, just a bit, not behind us though, but in front of us, leading us along a narrow path to another possible, more viable future. This door, if it is not already closed to us, is the door to the heart that takes the facts of our lives today, dreadful as they may be, and transforms them into experiences that can begin to relate us to the contours of our modern world as produced by a real phenomenon. Language, as a *phenomenon* can indeed speak to us and leave its message inscribed in our hearts, initiating us into the reality of our times so that its factual nature is transformed into the modern truth of our being today, through our suffering the reigning power of Being in its modern form.

The shift from merely using instrumental language to experiencing that same language as a living "alien" other, that is seeking us out, that wants something of us (rather than our using IT to get what we want) effectively turns a world inside out. Here is a dream-vision I had in the 90's that can illuminate the matter:

A man was among us and he looked quite normal, like the actor in 'Cocoon' except he was alien. He was friendly, wanted to, needed to, live amongst us, and was warmly welcomed. Many therapists were excited and thrilled with the glamour of his gifts, which included space ships that could fly at dizzying speeds. I joined in with this madness for a bit but lost interest and instead grew increasingly alarmed.

I tried to warn others, saying, 'What if ... what if ...' I decided to act; I wanted to burn him and raced around looking for a flame thrower. Instead I kept grabbing fire extinguishers and sprayed him with those ... useless. He tried to stop me and we seemed to realize that there was nothing personal in this. He wanted simply to live here and yet I could sense incredible danger to us. I said, "It's just that our species can't survive if you stay. We need to survive too!" Then I went back to my frantic search. He said, responding to my 'what ifs ...': "Do you mean, what if I spit on the carpet, or people?" And he did so, thus at last revealing the danger. A terrible poison was in his spittle, it dissolved flesh leaving horrible forms, like a fly dissolves its meal. I get more frantic until ..." (a long second part follows)[66]

As long as the inner/outer disjunction remains determinative of our thinking, connecting such a dream ("inner") as this to language and, in particular, instrumental language ("outer"), is futile. I underwent many initiatory experiences over a period of twenty years, breaking down this disjunction and opening my eyes to a new reality whose contours do not depend on it. Spontaneous connections could occur in my thinking and I could thus "perceive" my dream as *language* speaking to me: instrumental or technological language, initiating me into its reality as a phenomenon, revealing its nature to me.[67]

It was truly an ordeal for me, with considerable suffering involved over a number of years. At the same time, I was freed from instrumentality, from merely *using* language for my own purposes to being used by language for *its* purposes, just as poet might be used! In fact over this same period of time, poetic speech burst from me, geyser-like.[68] In one such poem, this following stanza occurs:

what kind of speech what words
form a fiery meteor arcing through the sky
with immense crackling power?

DREAMS AND THE INELUCTABLE BODY

C. G. Jung reports a clear example of the anomaly I am addressing here in my book. On two occasions he accurately interprets a dream (psychic phenomenon) solely in terms of physiological or empirical reality, i.e. he offers a medical diagnosis that was subsequently confirmed. In this essay I show how Jung's attempts to explain the success of his diagnosis are no more successful that Freud's attempts to explain why sometimes a cigar has no symbolical meaning, ("sometimes a cigar is just a cigar"). How we are to know when a dream refers to outer reality or to inner reality remains as deep a mystery as it was in Jung's time, as long as our language is determined by the inner/outer binary.

Ineluctable: not to be avoided or escaped. Latin: *eluctari*: to struggle out of; *luctari* to struggle.

American Heritage Dictionary

Can dreams help us with pressing questions of the ineluctable body—questions of illness, or even death and dying? I say "ineluctable body" to make clear that I am referring to the body that we each *have*, the body that is the object of current medical practice —the body that in times of health we can more or less ignore while we attend to matters of the mind, matters that now form the basis of most of our current cultural practices.

Someone once remarked that, in the times of our ancestors, the only worthwhile cultural practices were those of a ritual nature (birth, fertility, death, hunting, for example). The rest of the time, nothing much happened. Now in modern times, our situation is completely reversed. All our energies are directed towards practices that predominately occupy our conscious minds in some way, while once central practices ritually engaging the body are given only minimal attention, before we return to what is really important, the conscious mind and its correlative cultural practices.[69]

I am not persuaded that the popular cultural practices of professional sports, or athletics, are equivalent to past rituals of the body. I would still claim that these, too, are *primarily* practices of the mind, or more specifically the will! We seek to bring the ineluctable body under our complete control, no matter what it wants to do or what its limitations are, i.e., the body understood as a vehicle for the will.[70] The most highly valorized moments in sports occur when the intentions of the will overcome the limitations of the body (focus, eye on the ball, threading the eye of the needle, overcoming pain, etc.)

Yet this body, which we seek to bend to our will as a captain commands his ship and all on board, in turn, at times, commands our undivided attention. We most often are drawn to the ineluctable body when something goes wrong. The dominant cultural practice that we turn to when something goes wrong is of course modern medicine, which has a sophisticated arsenal of diagnostic procedures and treatment practices that are tested, reliable, and standardized, in accord with the measurable, universal features of the ineluctable body. The diagnosis and treatment of certain cancers for example are completely standardized with predictable, statistically measured outcomes.[71]

The provenance of such standardized medical procedures, based as they are on measurement, predictability, statistics, is of course science, or rather, the scientific mind. Modern medical practice privileges the mind, like most other practices today, even though medical practice focuses on the body. But *does* it focus on the body? Yes, anyone who has gone through painful surgery (as I have) can testify to the harsh reality of surgical interventions, but such an obvious empirical fact does not impair my claim that modern medicine is yet another modern cultural practice that privileges the mind and its abstract thinking. The ineluctable body only appears to the medical mind *as represented*, from which representation calculations and then procedures can follow. Any aspect of the body that cannot be so represented and measured simply does not exist for the medical profession. A person can feel terrible pain but if nothing shows up on the CAT scan or ultrasound, or remembered categories of thought, or explorative surgery (based on a hypothesis of the problem), for example, then the medical profession no longer knows what to do.

So, although modern medicine is the cultural practice of choice for millions when it comes to attending to the demands of the ineluctable body, it turns out that its fantastic success is not based on intimate direct knowledge of the body but on how well or accurately that body is represented to the scientific mind. The amazing advances in 3-D MRIs today bear testimony to the lengths we are willing to go to accurately represent the body to the mind in order to bring the ineluctable body under the control of the will once more. We could also think of the increasing number of delicate operations that are computer–driven with the surgeon's eyes completely focused on the computer screen digital representation of the body part while his scalpel is inside the body (I had one of those operations).

The pre-eminent cultural practice that focuses on the mind *as such* is of course depth psychology. And depth psychology is vitally concerned with the mind-body problem.[72] C. G. Jung was a pioneer in exploring this question and nowhere was this question more vexing, more problematic, than in his scant research on dreams and their relationship to the ineluctable body. In fact little progress has been made since his early research in the 1930's. I am aware of his work on synchronicity; the concept of "psychoid" and his theoretical search for an underlying unity (in theory) of psychic reality and empirical reality, the continuing work on "subtle body" that practitioners in dream work such as Arnold Mindell and Robert Bosnak are developing, following the hints left by Jung, and so on.

As valiant and worthwhile as these efforts are, there remains the reality of the ineluctable body, which is so often immune to such efforts. Bosnak for example makes no claims about the ontological status of "embodied dreams" or subtle bodies, being content with the phenomenologist's perspective:

> First I must reiterate that my attitude aspires to be phenomenal. I am not a metaphysician. I do not know of what Berthe's bull [an appearance in waking time of a dream bull—my insert] consists. I know nothing of his substance or if he is made of spirit. All I know is that he is present. From the phenomenal point of view the bull is an encountered embodied presence behaving like an intelligence alien to Berthe's. All I know about him is that he presents himself to Berthe as a living being … she has knowledge of the bull in the Biblical sense: visceral, erotic, initiatory, epiphanic[73]

This humble analysis by an experienced practitioner of depth psychology and dream work is very revealing of the problematic I am discussing here and so I can introduce some of its features by reference to Bosnak's quote. The most significant aspect of the quote and of Bosnak's methodology occurs when he speaks of being phenomenal. He is referring not to himself as perceiving a phenomenon (a dream "bull" appearance in waking time) but to his client (Berthe) who alone apperceives the "bull" phenomenon. *She* is the phenomenologist in that moment of apperception.

Bosnak's sensitive facilitation is aimed at developing

the faculty of the phenomenologist in the client. The emergence of the phenomenon, when it happens, is "explained" descriptively as a "ubiquitous spontaneous ability of memory to flashback into previous events" coming into play.[74] When he speaks of Berthe's encounter with the bull, the viscerality, eroticism, living quality, bull-presence—all these phenomenal qualities, along with memory, are available to Berthe only, and this fact marks the whole experience as one solely of the imagination or of poetic language, not to be confused with empirical reality or the ineluctable body at all. The only kind of bull that belongs to empirical reality would be a real bull whose presence would be shared quite publicly.

I personally have had several experiences of this kind, and the "body" that Bosnak and I are talking about in reference to such compelling appearances is quite different from what I call the ineluctable body.[75] While he makes legitimate claims about instances of emotional and *physical* healing (i.e. the kind of healing that medicine engages in), his methodology cannot be calculated, measured, or standardized like medicine, and he cannot (and does not) make any claims of physically healing people. In fact, his way of accounting for such physical healing, i.e. the "ubiquitous spontaneous ability of memory …" has all the phenomenology of a miracle or at least a placebo effect.

If the spontaneous "visceral" and "tangible" presence of a memory does not appear, then no healing occurs, as must have happened many times. Bosnak's use of language: "visceral", "physical", "tangible", in no way must be confused with the way those words are used in relation to the ineluctable body where they are *publicly* verifiable empirical phenomena. In his and other dream workers' (i.e. *mind* workers) practice, only the patient has access to such "materiality" proving that such practices are indeed working within the "sensual" reality of imagination, mind, or language and therefore not within actuality or the empirical reality of the ineluctable body, which most often remains, apart from miracles as I said, quite immune to such "mind-oriented" work.[76]

This is why I insist on the designation, "ineluctable"!

Jung however gives us some clues of his early interest in this body and his continued puzzlement, even vexation, concerning whether dreams (mind stuff) could refer to such a body (i.e. the body we each have, the empirical body that we submit to our will until it makes its independent demands on us, mainly through breakdown or illness, pain etc.) It's no accident that Jung should be so interested. He was both a medical doctor whose sole domain of interest is the ineluctable body as I have said, *and* a pioneer in the study of the psyche, purely from the psyche's point of view (the domain *per se* of depth psychology).

While he well knew that dreams are soul phenomena, by which we may hear psyche's speech, its immanent relations, its self-transformations, he also asked if a dream (or psyche, really) does or even can address the very different reality of the ineluctable body.

Let's now turn to Jung and follow his lead into what is surely no less a problematic now, some fifty years after his death.

Circa 1935, one Dr. Davie sent Jung a patient's dream. Davie reports that, "it would be of interest to submit this dream to Jung to ask what his interpretation would be." He sent only the dream, i.e. no case history or preliminary diagnosis. He no doubt experienced some shock when Jung replied with a correct medical diagnosis of a blockage in the cerebrospinal fluid. Here is the reported dream:

> Someone beside me kept on asking me something about oiling some machinery. Milk was suggested as the best lubricant. Apparently I thought that oozy slime was preferable. Then a pond was drained, and amid the slime there were too extinct animals. One was a minute mastodon. I forget what the other one was. [77]

In discussing this case, Jung was asked about the connection between the mind and the brain. He acknowledges the "controversial problem of psycho-physical parallelism for which I know of no answer, because it is beyond the reach of man's cognition … the psychic fact and the physiological fact come together in a peculiar way … We see them as two on account of the utter incapacity of our mind to think them together. Because of that possible unity of the two things, we must expect to find dreams that are more on the physiological side than on the psychological …"

When Jung was pressed on how he arrived at his startling conclusion that the dream referred to a medical condition of the body, he demurred saying, "[t]o explain what the mastodon really means in an organic respect and why I must take that dream as an organic symptom would start an argument that you would accuse me of the most terrible obscurantism." Later on in the same passage Jung appeals to the possession of a "special knowledge" (symbology, comparative mythology, etc.) that set him apart from his medical colleagues of the time saying only that the acquisition of this knowledge ("of the apparatus of parallelism") is necessary to help the physician make judgments whether "this dream is organic and that one is not." This discussion then leads to Jung's view of synchronicity as the central concept for addressing the problematic of a supposed unity of mind and brain.

It is easy to imagine that his professional colleagues would be left impressed with the undeniable correctness of his medical interpretation of the dream but no less befuddled about how he arrived at such a conclusion and about whether there was any generalizability in his method. They may also have felt diminished by Jung's comparison to the medieval mind if it were faced with the complexity of scientific advancements.

But if we consult some of Jung's texts around the same time, and later, when he addressed the same problematic, it seems that, for all his "superiority" in the matter of offering psycho-physical parallelism as an explanatory principle, Jung was almost as completely in the dark as his interlocutors of 1935. He appeared to have little or no adequate account of how he came to his correct medical diagnosis in this particular case.

We can see evidence of this startling conclusion in a statement Jung made some twenty years later (1952), in a letter to Smythies, where he refers to:

... the peculiar fact that on the one hand consciousness has so exceedingly little direct information of the body from within, and that on the other hand the unconscious (i.e., dreams and other products from the "unconscious") refers very rarely to the body and, if it does, it is always in the most roundabout way, i.e., through highly "symbolized" images. For a long time I have considered this fact as negative evidence for the existence of a subtle body or at least for a curious gap between mind and body. Of a psyche dwelling in its own body one should expect at least that it would be immediately and thoroughly informed of any change of conditions therein. Its not being the case demands some explanation. [78]

We can also see the same problematic appearing an earlier discussion (c. 1933) following another correct medical diagnosis by Jung subsequent to hearing a young girl's dreams. He reports the dreams of this patient:

I was coming home night. Everything is as quiet as death. The door into the living room is half open, and I see my mother hanging from the chandelier, swinging to and fro in the cold wind that blows in through the open windows. Another time I dreamt that's a terrible noise broke out in the house at night. I get up and discover that frightened horse is tearing through the rooms. At last it finds the door into the hall, and jumps through the hall window from the fourth floor into the street below. I was terrified when I saw it lying there all, mangled. [79]

After a lengthy exploration of the main symbols in the dreams, that of "mother" and "horse," Jung concludes that "both dreams point to a grave organic disease with a fatal outcome. This prognosis was soon confirmed." Again we can see a lengthy, purely psychological analysis producing an empirical (medical) conclusion, and again Jung does not adequately tell us how he arrived at it. He does argue his case in this way: He notes that there is a link between the dream mother and horse in that they both commit suicide. He then proceeds to analyze each symbol in terms of their meaning, concluding, "the unconscious life is destroying itself ... the animal life is destroying itself."

In the course of this argument, Jung slides effortlessly from a discussion of *psychic* reality (unconscious life) to one of *empirical* reality (animal life) by making confused "category" claims. In another example he claims that "mother" first refers to an archetype (psychic reality), then refers to the place of origin, to nature, to that which passively creates, to materiality, the womb, the vegetative functions (all these references are to empirical or external reality) ... the nature-bound life of the body (external reality) ... the unconscious (back to psychic reality), the psychological foundations of consciousness (psychic reality again). He continues in like-fashion with the symbol of the horse: "horse" referring now to the animal life of the body (empirical reality), and now to the unconscious (psychic reality), and now to the animal impulses (empirical reality), etc.

Nowhere in this confusion of categories of thought does Jung tell us when we should stop referring to "mother," "earth," "body," or "materiality" (the quotes indicating that the reference is now to language, psyche, imagination, or mind) and start thinking referentially to mother, earth, body, materiality, our vegetative system, as categories of externality. He simply does so willy-nilly throughout the text as he tries to understand his own thought processes leading to his correct diagnosis.

As Jung's letter to Smythies shows twenty years later, Jung could never find a satisfactory answer to this problematic of the relationship between psychic reality and actuality or empirical reality.

And neither can we, some fifty years later.

There is another way to understand what is at stake in the attempt to refer a dream to an organic condition in general. This way concerns the relationship between language and nature in its historical aspect. Jung was a physician who was familiar with the Latin names for organs of the body. The practice of naming organs with Latin names is said to have originated with Vesalius in the 16th century.[80] Vesalius' naming was based on unaided sensory perceptions of the organ in question, rather than its abstract chemistry or molecular structure, as is the preferred case today.

The pituitary gland was so named because of its sensory quality of sliminess; the mammillary bodies of the hypothalamus were so named for their visual form which resembles breasts with nipples; the hypothalamus lies under (hypo) the thalamus, deep within the brain, which must have appeared to the naming researcher as an inner chamber, even bedroom, where new life may begin (a nerve seems to originate there medically); ventricles were named for their ready appearance as hollow cavities, and so on. What is happening here in this naming?

The imagination of the researcher was ignited by the

aesthetic or sensory quality of the organ under investigation. Vesalius then found language, a proper name, to refer to the appearance. The word was also meant to *resemble* the object in the sense that the form of the word (as image) was intended to imitate that of the actual natural object, without however, the researcher necessarily making any such conscious distinction between image and empirical reality at all. He simply named the organ with the "best-fitting" Latin word. At the time of Vesalius, language and reality were distinct but not yet disjunctive as they are today, so that an implicit identity still existed between word and reality.[81] Under this logical determination of knowledge, what was said about the word was also what could be said about the body (for example).[82]

Jung was obviously familiar with the Latin names for anatomical organs, being a physician but more than this obvious connection with his professional contemporaries and tradition, Jung was equally familiar with the fact that words come laden with latent historical meaning, which can be uncovered by appropriate methods (etymology, history of symbols, comparative mythology, hermeneutics), and released into consciousness.

When given the dream, as a physician and depth psychologist, Jung's imagination could immediately connect the Latin names of the dream images (mastodon, slime, milk, pond, lubricant) with the anatomical parts of the brain that are named by similar figures of speech. For example, "mastodon" means "breast-teeth," and the name "mammillary" bodies, associated with the hypothalamus, carries an image of the breast. For a moment Jung's mind shared the same logical structure of consciousness as Vesalius. The modern day logic of disjunction or difference, gave way to the more participatory form of consciousness of resemblances and thus what is true of language is also true of "reality". He could thus imaginatively perceive the body aesthetically, linguistically, as Vesalius did outwardly, and, emerging from that temporary status of participatory consciousness, he could then offer a modern medical diagnosis.

The question of method now sharpens to the following formulation, which can be generalized from the particulars of this one dream to the question of dream interpretation in general—the question that Jung could not answer during the course of his entire life ("I know of no answer, because it is beyond the reach of man's cognition") i.e. how to know when to interpret a dream in terms of the natural world or empirical reality or in terms of the psychic or world of imagination (immanent relations). This formulation has a surprising historical root, one that seems to still affect our understanding of the inner/outer polarity, since its (the historical root's) inception in the 18th and 19th centuries. This root goes by the popular name of Romanticism.

Romanticism is synonymous with the discovery of the imagination, *as such*! This discovery was accompanied by a renewed emphasis on natural objects: "an abundant imagery with an equally abundant quantity of natural objects, such is the fundamental ambiguity that characterizes the poetics of Romanticism. The tension between the two polarities never ceases to be problematic."[83] According to de

Man, the discovery of the imagination *per se* led to a poetics in which the imagination was conceived or understood in terms of natural processes, while at the same time the *reality* of the imagination as such was beginning to be understood as being fundamentally different from that of natural processes. De Man explores this difference through a difficult deconstruction of the rhetoric of one of Hölderlin's poems comparing the origin of poetic language to that of flowers. He demonstrates that Hölderlin's metaphor fails with the consequence that poetic speech must find its own mode of becoming, namely "out of nothing," unlike the real flower which originates in the transcendental idea, Flower (this being the Platonic implications of Hölderlin's own rhetoric, and not an insertion of de Man's metaphysics).

This means that poetic words, language, the imagination, are distinct from natural entities, "Poetic language can do nothing but originate over and over and over again; it is always constitutive; able to posit ... but unable to give a foundation to what it posits except as an intent of consciousness. The word is always a free presence of the mind."[84]

This is the monumental, only partially realized, discovery of Romanticism! It seems that, with the discovery of the imagination, ambivalence emerges that even today has not been settled, as we will see in regards to dream interpretation. Poetic language seeks to draw closer to, or imitate the ontological status of the natural object (concrete, "sensual" figures, or "subtle bodies" for example) while at the same time insisting on its own reality status *as* imagination:

At times, romantic thought and romantic poetry seem to come so close to giving in completely to the nostalgia for the object that it becomes difficult to distinguish between object and image, between imagination and perception, between an expressive or constitutive and mimetic or literal language. [85]

De Man draws from romantic sources to show how many serious attempts were made to think the imagination in terms of natural processes by, for example, fusing matter and imagination or by amalgamating perception and reveries, as Bachelard has done, for example:

> Critics who speak of a "happy relationship" between matter and consciousness fail to realize that the very fact that the relationship has to be established within the medium of language indicates that it does not exist in actuality. [86]

He then goes on to show that other romantic poetry points to a completely different conception of the imagination, marking the possibility for consciousness to exist independently of all relationship with the outside world, coming into full play when the "light of the sense goes out". He adds, "[w]e know very little about the kind of images that such an imagination would produce, except they would have little in common with what we have come to expect from familiar metaphorical figures."[87]

De Man does not leave us completely in the dark, however. He describes the phenomenology of the imagination, conceived as a new and distinct mode of being from that of natural being, as revealed by the great Romantic poets, such as Wordsworth, Rousseau, and Hölderlin:

> The ontological priority, housed at first in the earthly and pastoral "flower" has been transposed into an entity that could still, if one wishes, be called "nature" but could no longer be equated with matter, objects, earth, stones, or flowers … the poetic imagination tears itself away, as it were, from a terrestrial nature and moves forward to this "other nature" … associated with the diaphanous, limpid, and immaterial quality of a light that dwells nearer to the skies … the transparency of the air represents the perfect fluidity of a mode of being that has moved beyond the power of earthly things. [88]

This rather difficult analysis of the rhetoric of Romanticism is necessary to understand the problematic that Jung "inherited" as he struggled with "… the peculiar fact that on the one hand consciousness has so exceedingly little direct information of the body from within, and that on the other hand the unconscious (i.e., dreams and other products from the "unconscious") refers very rarely to the body and, if it does, it is always in the most roundabout way, i.e., through highly "symbolized" images."[89]

With this informing background in mind let's now return to Jung and his dream interpretation.

Jung's interpretive work on the dream stayed within the realm of the imagination and language, from start to finish, as I tried to show in my reconstruction of his method. His final interpretation could only follow one of two available paths given us from our Romantic heritage. He could, like many authors informed by the Romantic turn, draw closer to natural processes on the assumption that the imagination represents natural processes, leading to an external interpretation (medical diagnosis); or he could regard the imagination as a reality comprising immanent relations only, having no necessary connection at all with external reality. In this case, his interpretation would remain one concerning the psyche and its self-movement (a purely "inner" interpretation, if you will).

This ambiguity or even aporia in the Romantic text concerning the ontology of the imagination shows that Jung's choice of an external interpretation of the dream cannot be determined by the text of the dream at all. The text reveals the Romantic ambiguity concerning the nature of the imagination! This is why Jung could give his colleagues no assistance in working out when to interpret a dream in terms of natural processes (like disease) and when to remain psychological. He has to make a choice that cannot be determined by *any* dream text because its essentially linguistic nature has to contain the historically unresolved (maybe unresolvable) ambiguity in the reality status of the imagination and its relationship to empirical reality.

There is no way to decide, on the basis of the given dream text, even though Jung's medical diagnosis was correct. Jung didn't know how he arrived at those impressive and correct empirical diagnoses from an analysis of imaginative or poetic language (or psychological interpretation), beyond some strange intellectual idea like "psychoid." [90]

We cannot get out of the historical determinants into which we are born, just like that. The Romantic vision of the imagination, with its ambiguity of reference, continues to inform our thinking about the vexed relationship between mind and the ineluctable body. The Romantics were struggling to come to terms with a breath-taking transformation taking place in our reality principle. The imagination (psyche) was breaking free of its moorings in nature and beginning to experience itself as a mode of being quite distinct from that of nature, as de Man describes, creating the gap between consciousness and the body that so befuddled the older Jung. Owen Barfield puts it this way:

> We *live* in that abrupt gap between matter and spirit; we exist by virtue of it as autonomous, self-conscious individual spirits, as free beings. Often, in addition, it makes us feel lamentably isolated. But because our freedom and responsibility depend on it, any way that involves disregarding the gap, or pretending it is not there, is a way we take at our peril. [91]

It seems to me that, given this gap as a starting point to any further research, a good deal of preparation can proceed with a kind of scouring procedure, making the necessary distinctions between categories of thought: those that belong to the realm of the imagination and those that belong to empirical reality or the ineluctable body. I have tried to point out this necessity here in reference to Jung's confused (confusion of categories) modern explanations of his "organic" dream interpretations.

After having established our given reality status today, Barfield then goes on to propose two directions that become possible from the acknowledgement of the gap: "We shall be free to turn either outward towards what we perceive [natural objects—my insert] or inward towards what we *are*." He elaborates with historical examples:

> It will be in the former direction that we shall turn, as Goethe did, when our primary concern is to have to do with spirit through nature, And, by perceiving nature as expression [of spirit—my insert], to realize for ourselves that matter is after all spirit. It will be in the latter direction that we shall turn, as Hegel did, when our primary concern is to have to do with the human spirit. [92]

I want to conclude this essay by taking Barfield's path into nature (Goethe's direction) and asking, with a twist, what would nature, or more specifically the ineluctable body, look like today if we *could* perceive it as an expression of spirit, now that the body and all things spiritual or psychic are governed by the logic of difference (i.e., disjunctive)?[93]

This question involves calling up a third historical figure who found his way, from the gap as it were, to a new formulation of reality, an inception, disclosing a hitherto unheard-of world where the "things" may appear now as expressions of spirit, including the former ineluctable body of medical science. Though this figure is well known and famous for his other discoveries, this particular one has not been noticed. Yet it may one day be understood as an inception, disclosing a new world of appearances.

This figure is, yes, C. G. Jung, and his momentous yet little noticed or understood discovery (even by him) may be found from within the text of The Red Book![94]

The formulation of the inner/outer, imagination/ nature disjunction could be said in literary terms as a clear separation between fictional reality and empirical reality. We know that fiction refers to itself and has its own rules of rhetoric, syntax, etc. while empirical reality refers to real historical or outer events, i.e. things in the world. This too-easy distinction is now in the process of completely breaking down under the onslaught of insightful and penetrating literary criticism, deconstruction, philosophical analysis, and courageous artists willing to undergo the breakdown in traditional categories, etc. As I have shown elsewhere we may see a living example of this breakdown in categories of thought, normally kept well apart, as the very text of The Red Book, a record of Jung's *experience* of the breakdown in literary and ontological categories.

The core of Jung's experiences during his "confrontation with the unconscious" lay in a sustained experience of "suspension," during which he was initiated into a reality that lies "beyond" the present imagination/nature disjunction, along with its "gap".[95] This initiation opened his eyes to a new set of appearances as the natural world. There was no longer a disjunction between inner/outer or imagination and nature.

The details of this transformation can be found in my essay.[96] I formulate the new reality prosaically and inadequately as an interpenetration of fictional reality and empirical reality but it is better named as a figure of speech, such as "the coming guest."[97] By this I mean that fictional reality now gains a reality equal to our presently privileged empirical reality and begins to interpenetrate that reality, destroying both previous categories that maintain the "gap".

Jung's period of suspension occurred in 1912-c1920

and shaped the man Jung. His initiation into the new reality opened his eyes to fresh perceptions of the appearances, and could also account for his astonishing medical diagnosis of what is for us the ineluctable body. This body, along with the rest of "dead" nature is what remains after the imagination departs nature into its own quite distinct mode of being. The ineluctable body is a natural object of perception without imagination, as matter only, if you like.

It seems to me that the imagined anatomical organs of the ineluctable body became transparent to spirit for Jung, enabling him to make his diagnosis. He was able to perceive the organs as images, or figures of speech: the image of the mastodon, the slime, the pond, etc. For this world of appearances, it is no longer of any interest whether Jung saw the actual brain of the patient externally or whether he carried out his research inwardly, because the categories of externality and interiority have been overcome.

I rather suspect that some medical Intuitives proceed in a similar manner. They are given clinical data and can visualize the organs as images, colors, or some such, and then know how to interpret what they perceive in a way helpful to the more prosaic medical practitioner.

The confusion around the mind/body problem continues today well beyond Jung and depth psychology. It goes to the core of neuroscience and the "hard problem of consciousness". We are trying to conceptually cross a gap using categories of thought that generate the gap in the first place. This why neither Jung nor anyone since could understand how he arrived at a medical diagnosis from a dream. This difficulty in understanding points to a fundamental problematic of our times and we cannot solve this problem in the terms that produce it. Only an initiatory process will do and human beings of course cannot will that to happen. Individuals can instead be called into participation with the transformational movements of the background logical determinants of our existence, just as Jung was during his confrontation with the unconscious. Such initiations open the eyes to new appearances, as I have said, from which can follow the slow cultural work of making new language that can adequately carry the new perceptions into actuality through some art form.

We now *have* the ineluctable body but this has the potential to arise as a new body, one which is expressive of spirit, as an image, in earthly existence! We can get hint of how this "new body" can arise by reference to a poem by Wordsworth.[98] Although he is speaking of a landscape in this sonnet, the shift from mere perception of surfaces (or literalism) to imaginative perception of depth within nature is analogous to what I am suggesting here in relation to the ineluctable body and the new body.

I will ask you to imagine a still lake reflecting the stars, all very literal until he asks, "Is it a mirror?—or the nether Sphere/opening to view the abyss ..." This line occurs as the activity of the imagination suddenly penetrates the surface perception and reveals a domain normally hidden by the light of day. He then hears a voice speak and address him. But he has not departed nature; he is viewing the same scene with the eyes of the imagination. In fact his vision is dual: the literal has

not gone away and the symbolic has opened up within
the literal:

> Clouds, lingering yet, extend in solid bars
> Through the grey west; and lo! these waters, steeled
> By breezeless air to smoothest polish, yield
> A vivid repetition of the stars;
> Jove, Venus, and the ruddy crest of Mars
> Amid his fellows beauteously revealed
> At happy distance from earth's groaning field,
> Where ruthless mortals wage incessant wars.
> Is it a mirror?—or the nether Sphere
> Opening to view the abyss in which she feeds
> Her own calm fires?—But list! a voice is near;
> Great Pan himself low-whispering through the reeds,
> 'Be thankful, thou; for, if unholy deeds
> Ravage the world, tranquillity is here!

DROUGHT, OR THE WASTELAND

I wrote this essay in response to a conference call for papers in 2015. The conference was oriented to solving very real problems in a drought-stricken world. I "heard" a call within the word "call" and decided to follow that call. The implicit inwardness or interiority of the empirically real "drought" opened up for me. Drought now became wasteland, a poetic figure of speech (i.e., "inner reality"). But still, drought and wasteland are determined by the inner/outer binary. A memory was released, of a dream-vision I had many years ago. This dream-vision burst into appearance as an anomaly, as the inner/outer disjunction went under. Through the horror I gained a glimpse of a way through the drought/wasteland, and decided to follow it ...

The aim of this online conference is a "global call for community solutions" to the pressing issue of drought, and contributions may draw from four major disciplines, or areas of knowledge: Science, Business, Politics, and Spirit. The editors encourage a broad range of presentation styles, e.g., interviews, letters, poems, posts, mud, pictures …

This generous "outreach" to the community implies that the time for privileging experts or authority figures is over and we are entering an historical moment when we need to tap into something deeper in our being, something wiser, accessible to all.

The *call* for community solutions may be heard as a call to arms, or a call to action: "something must be done!" But, since words convey far more than the surface content of the message, I think it is prudent to develop an ear for the deeper, historical tones that work quietly, even determinatively within the very ordinary words we use to communicate our conscious concerns to one another. This buried or unconscious history in language shapes and informs our real actions in the world much more than does the information we communicate in familiar ways. Because our linguistic heritage lays "hidden", or unconscious, *as the within-ness* of language, we usually only encounter it, at first, as our perceptions of the real world. The world is a real appearance to us, but its appearance, its contours if you like, is an expression of those long-forgotten meanings in our language. What we have "forgotten", through force of habitual usage of words, now appears in front of us, as the contours of the real world, but crucially, having no felt connection to us anymore.

For example, we easily perceive the parabolic arc that any object thrown in the air follows in its journey back to earth. But, before Galileo transformed the core meaning of motion, our ancestors perceived a very different trajectory, not parabolic at all, more like a curve for a while, then, straight down. This trajectory was a real appearance to them and we all had to be "taught", through the new concept, how to see the parabolic curve as the new, real appearance of trajectories. As this new perception became a habit, Galileo's revolutionary *concept* of motion that gives rise to the parabolic curve became lost to us and it now lies deep in the history of our language, within the meaning of the commonly used word, motion. We now simply perceive the world as it is: a world in which objects follow parabolic paths.[99]

We can likewise turn our historical imagination to the little examined, but often-used word, "call", as in "a call for community solutions."[100] What historical determinants lie within our unconscious usage of this word, shaping our perceptions of the world, quite independently of our conscious intentions? If we can allow these "roots of meaning" to rise to the surface, how will they affect our discourse re: drought and the present condition of the real world? What action could follow from such an inquiry, i.e. action that matters?

At bottom, "call" surprisingly hides an ancient meaning of screaming, shrieking. [101] Moving "up" through history we also encounter more recent meanings of naming and visitor. Already, from this brief excursion into the historical depths of our being via language, we can see that, within our habitual, unconscious use of the common word "call", in relation to a world condition of drought, lie some deeper resonances at work, "behind the scenes" as it were, in our perceptions of the world-as-drought.[102] The psyche is thus quite involved in this call to community action, but her involvement may not be quite identical with the understandable sense of urgency we have today, that *we* need to do something, that we need to help the world somehow, in its present plight.

In our use of the word "call", we invoke buried images of shrieking, screaming, naming, and visitor, which can now rise up to the surface of consciousness from the depths of our linguistic being where, if we remain open, they can begin to stain our present consciousness, like an alchemical tincture.

We can now imaginatively ask, for example, *who* is screaming and shrieking, without needing to literalize the question by that old habit of thought, or trope—the inner/outer disjunction. If we do succumb to the trope, then we can only conclude that we humans are literally shrieking or screaming, or alternatively, that the world is poetically "screaming" for our help. This familiar move betrays Being, which is no longer concerned with the truth of such disjunctions as inner/outer, as Nietzsche demonstrates so forcefully in his opus.[103] To serve Being today, it is more important that we *receive* the shrieking and screaming as it comes to us from our and the world's mutual depths of being. This may be in fact what we are here to do, as Rilke teaches through the example of his own life:

Since I still don't know enough about pain,
This terrible darkness makes me small.
If it's you, though—
press down hard on me, break in
that I may know the weight of your hand,
and you the fullness of my cry.[104]
Or, as he says further on:
Are we, perhaps, here just for saying: House,
Bridge, Fountain, Gate, Jug, Olive tree, Window,—
Possibly: Pillar, Tower? … . But for saying, remember,
Oh, for such saying as never the things themselves
Hoped so intensely to be.[105]

Can we resonate with the screaming and shrieking long enough to hear its name, as it names itself to us, in the way that a visitor would introduce herself?

I had a dream recently in which a visitor called at my door. Children, light-hearted and laughing, accompanied it. This visitor rendered me mute. I could not name it. It has a shape of a cat's head that morphs into the body of a cassowary, an Australian bird from the emu family. This strange being came into my home and washed its face or mouth in a fountain. It was friendly and seemed to get what it wanted from our meeting. After the dream, I am still mute and must therefore wait until my marvelous visitor begins to speak through me, as its possible mouthpiece. It is not up to me to name it as if it belonged to my familiar world.

This visitor *could* appear to me only after decades of my dwelling in the "screaming and shrieking", following its first appearance in my life, at a time when I was living the kind of wasteland that T. S. Eliot's poem knows: [106]

What are the roots that clutch, what branches grow
Out of this stony rubbish? Son of man,
You cannot say, or guess, for you know only
A heap of broken images, where the sun beats,
And the dead tree gives no shelter, the cricket no
relief,
And the dry stone no sound of water. Only
There is shadow under this red rock,
(Come in under the shadow of this red rock),
And I will show you something different from either
Your shadow at morning striding behind you
Or your shadow at evening rising to meet you;
I will show you fear in a handful of dust.[107]

While we normally think that something has to be done to the wasteland in order to rescue it, or nourish it, I learned that the wasteland itself is the "place" of its own "cure", if we can stay long enough within it, and endure its message. And so, from within the drought came this life-changing, powerful, dream-vision:

I am working at a thermonuclear facility along with others. It is the central facility of our society. It is regulated and master-minded by a central computer, much like HAL in '2001', even to the detail of the red eye with which we could communicate. This computer is female. Everybody thought of her as an IT! In contrast I would look into her eye and talk to her, subject to subject, with love.

In other words, the feminine regulating principle which is the glue of society, by relating all parts to one another and to the whole has become an IT! But my response alone is not enough. Slowly the lack of relatedness begins to drive her mad with grief. At first, this madness shows up as an increasing, dangerous autonomy in the operation of the objects associated with the facility (society)—elevators going sideways, doors opening and shutting autonomously, etc. Then people begin to harm one another in various ways until the social system becomes frayed and anarchy increases, with civilization and its values losing cohesion and crumbling.

I find myself in a garbage dump, near the central facility. Some abandoned children give me a gun to kill them. I take it away from them. A vagabond is sitting in an abandoned car, sewing a boot for the coming (nuclear?) winter. He also used to work in the facility, he said. A sick woman careens by. A man tries to take his twin boys up a tower.

Then I am standing at the centre of the facility. It is Ground Zero. A large cleared area of gray sand and dirt with concentric rings, like a target, radiating from the centre. The ground is slightly raised at the centre, like a discus, sloping away to the edges. I sense that She is going to explode. I am right at the epicentre. She is going to destroy us all and this means Herself in an apocalypse of rage-despair, loathing, hate, and grief because of our stupidity. I must get away from the epicentre now. I sprint across the field, down the slight incline to the periphery of the field and sprawl prone, with my head facing the centre, just as she explodes.

The wind starts from the centre and blows out (in contrast to the natural phenomenon which sucks up). It begins as a breeze, increasing in strength and intensity until it becomes an unbearable shriek. Lying face down, I am sheltered by the slope as the wind rips over my back. But I mustn't raise my head at all— a few inches of protection and that's it! Then I know the shriek is hers.

I 'see' Her standing at the centre, and a poem bursts spontaneously out of me as I record the experience:

goddess
flowing
in her agony
awesome!
incomparable grief and rage
divine suffering
excruciating pain
such terrible agony
beauty, sublime beauty
how is love possible?
yet this is what i feel

A bubble of calm forms around me while the storm of destruction rages on outside. She is with me in a form that I can talk to, personally.

Then the bubble collapses and the wind/goddess shrieks again. Gradually it dissipates and as I turn over, feeling its last tendrils whip at my clothes, I find myself tumbling out of this apocalyptic scene into a city street, the everyday world of my daily life. I have been returned from a visionary place to my ordinary life.

Then, I wake up.[108]

This self-presentation of reality did indeed stain my being, like an alchemical tincture. I was brought to edge of suicide, over subsequent months. "Her" screaming and shrieking *became* mine, as it already was from the start, i.e., existing in the depths of being, beyond "mine" and "yours", beyond "inner" and "outer". How could I stand the given knowledge that Being itself, in the form of the goddess, has been consigned to oblivion, abandoned, for over 3000 years by the cultural encrustation that privileges the human subject and centuries-long imposition of its various "world-views" *on* Being? The goddess, ignored for so long, is now destroying that which she loves and in so doing, destroys herself. This knowledge "pressed down hard upon me," as Rilke says, and her rage-despair became the "fullness of my cry."

Yet the very same dreadful terror carries the "miraculous cure" within it. I was given a poem that worked performatively on me. "Incomparable grief and rage", if endured by the human recipient, will transform into love, and indeed did so, as I feverishly wrote with increasing astonishment. The *poesis* itself generated love from the depths of rage-despair, all within the human heart.

The "call" begins with shrieking and screaming, and reveals, decades later, an as-yet unnamed friendly visitor who calls upon me. Although this strange and wonderful being did not offer up a name, I am struck by the fact that it came as an animal figure. I can presently only conceive of this marvel in terms of a complex image: a cat's head and a cassowary's body. This presentation means that I do not yet know the "speech" of this (way of) being, coming to us from within the despair of the drought or nuclear wasteland.

My "visitor" dream shows there is a clear affinity between this new way of "animal being" and fountains of water. Does this suggest that the drought is brought to an end when we can politely receive the unknown visitor, without imposing yet another "world view" on its presence? Can we become more animal-like, in the way that van der Post advises, concerning bush manners

—knowing how to comport ourselves in the face of the unknown, friendly, but possibly dangerous (cassowaries have a lethal kick) "animal" presence?[109]

We are not only faced with literal droughts *in* the world; we are critically facing a world appearing *as* drought—a waterless wasteland, now filled only with a self-destructive rage-despair. The appearance of the strange "animal" visitor coincides with the appearance of a fountain—the end of the drought, if this strange being can be received as such by us.

We are presently faced with the end of one entire way of being, a way that has dominated for 3000 years, and the "call" heralds a new way of being. One of its "faces" is that of my dream visitor. To receive this visitor and end the drought is a task that begins with hearing and receiving the abyssal depths of our historical being, in the form of shrieks and screams— the agony of 3000 years of consignment to oblivion. If we can endure, suffer this rage-despair, as it works its will on us, then love may be born in our hearts, the kind of love that can prepare us to receive the next manifestation of being, the strange and wonderful "animal" presence. If we can restrain the Adamic impulse to *impose* a name on this wonderful being, then it may, in time, name itself to us, and in so doing … name us!

Returning now to the call for community solutions, what effective action may follow when the psychic determinants of our perceptions are brought into relationship to our conscious concerns? There is no compulsion to include *psychic* being as a factor in any analysis of our modern predicament. Most disciplines in fact proceed from a very different *a priori*. They assume that our present set of real appearances—a solid world exterior to human consciousness, having no consciousness of its own—has been the only one for all time. The corollary to this stance is that we humans are solely responsible for our present crisis and its solution —there is only us *human* beings![110]

Accepting *psychic* being (as distinguished from *human* being), as an *a priori*, is a choice and commitment, usually based on some convincing experience of the reality of the psyche, and not simply an ideological choice, based on personal preference. Once the commitment is made, we become open to what psyche may teach us in regards to the real world's *being* and our place in it.

My experiences with psychic reality have taught me, for example, that the drought, from psyche's point of view, though disturbingly real, is not simply some event exterior to me, and equally, "drought" is not simply a projected quality of my personal psychological situation onto the exterior world. Drought, or the wasteland, is the condition of the real world in its present *being*, at a depth shared by all of us. Once the human being goes to those depths and becomes a mouthpiece for the rage-despair that lies there, then the world's being may "speak" through, and *as*, its human representative. Such "speech" may take the form of "art", new modes of discourse, or cultural forms that can reflect a new human-world configuration.[111] As this new configuration manifests through the creative efforts of many individuals, a correspondingly new set of real appearance will arise, an inceptive moment that, as

Heidegger says, will inaugurate an entirely new history.

THE NIGHT OF THE RAT:
A Soul Phenomenological Approach to Synchronicity

THE PLAYERS

A highly distressed married couple came to see my partner and me for Joint Couples Therapy. She had discovered his decades-long infidelities only "by accident"—finding unknown phone numbers, links to websites in his smart phone, or questioning his unusual activities. His vehement denials, protests, "gaslighting" (they were "meaningless encounters" etc.) had the initial effect of shaking her grip on reality and they both had commenced therapy with the agreed aim of helping her get better with medications, along with her individual therapy. In other words her depression needed help as she should be over it by now and they should be able to move on together as he clearly wanted.

When they finally came to see my partner and me for couples therapy, we began to challenge this toxic mutually held view of her as identified patient. A good deal of our therapeutic work consisted in supporting her intuitions, emotional responses and her realistic appraisals of his secret sexual activities, in terms of the disruption to their intimacy. Under her withering, accusatory, vengeful attacks, his belittling, dismissive, defensive posture began to break down. He became more frightened as the likely end of the marriage became more visible to him. His efforts of course then turned to the task of saving his marriage. He began to admit his guilt, as his lies and secrets were exposed by the careful prosecutory evidence she had accumulated (phone records, noting contradictions in his "testimony", witnesses, etc.) He became tearful, "remorseful", no longer able to continue the conman act. But my partner and me could see that all these conciliatory gestures had a deeper secret, motive—saving his marriage. The "con" continued. His partner's intense suffering was met with "empathic" attempts aimed at bringing the suffering to an end in order to save him from a broken family and divorce. He said and did anything to avoid that outcome—a matter of survival!

She had endured intense suffering by his secretive actions and subsequent denials, along with her refusal to trust her intuition, of course—turning away from what she "knew" so that her security and comfort could be preserved. She aimed at survival too! But he remained largely impervious to her suffering, remaining psychologically "outside" her agonies. He was not penetrated by the sight (wailing, rage, withdrawal, threats of leaving, etc.) of her violated soul—until one night when a powerful synchronicity shocked him out of his stance as isolated subject into an unexpected participation in their mutual suffering.

NIGHT OF THE RAT

They were watching an episode of a TV series which began to explore prostitution—interviews on the street. These images triggered her into her wound again and she angrily withdrew to bed. He followed her trying to make amends once more, to no avail. She was inconsolable and he was helpless ("what do you want me to do?" "Do whatever you want!") He crawled into bed and she continued her tirade of accusations. This dreadful discourse continued unabated until about 2am when they both heard a loud, chilling snap! He knew instantly what it was. A rat was caught in the trap he had laid down. "Go deal with it!" She shoved him out of bed. He went downstairs and was horrified by what he saw. The powerful trap caught part of the rat's head, exposing the brain as the rat continued to squeal and writhe in agony. He watched, paralysed, knowing there was nothing he could do, that he was responsible, having laid the trap, and now he had to deal with a horrible and grisly death.

When he told this story during our couples session, in great detail at my request, I asked him and his partner if they found any significance in the temporal co-incidence of their bitter fight late at night and the grotesque death of the rat. They did not and wanted to carry on with their discussion of their painful argument that night.

But I sensed a significance in his account of this temporal co-incidence of events, although I did not know why I did. I sensed the presence of a synchronicity in the telling of the events. Their bitter argument was now linguistically paired with the grotesque death of the rat! I am making an important distinction between the events-in-themselves that night having no connection with each other and the memory of those events as told to us, in which they had became paired as a synchronicity. In other words, neither of the players was struck at the time of the incident by a pairing of any events. The phenomenon of a synchronistic pairing only occurred in the subsequent telling of the incident during our session. Furthermore, the only person who was struck by that pairing was me!

I waited until they had exhausted their well-established discourse of attack and "atonement" and then I approached their story of the incident again, following which the session took an unexpected turn. But I don't want to get ahead of myself here. There is some preliminary work to do first.

WHAT IS SYNCHRONICITY?

C. G. Jung understood synchronicity as a temporal co-incidence of inner and outer events that cannot be understood causally but remains meaningful. What he means here by "meaningful" is that the co- including inner and outer events, even a series of them, share an implicit meaning, as in this example from Jung:

> Today is Friday. We have fish for lunch. Somebody happens to mention the custom of making an "April fish" of someone…in the afternoon, a former patient of mine, whom I had not seen for months, showed me some extremely impressive pictures of fish which she had painted in the meantime. In the evening I was showing a piece of embroidery with fish-like sea-monsters in it. On the morning of April 2 another patient, whom I have not seen for many years, told me a dream in which she stood on the shore of a lake and saw a large fish that swim straight towards her and landed at her feet. I was at this time engaged on a study of fish symbol in history…[112]

I am calling the principle Jung is suggesting here the principle of *resemblance of form*. Nothing mystifying, and nothing to do with anyone's subjective reaction to the co-incidence, such as Jung's reaction to this "run of events" which "seemed to me to have a certain numinous quality," as he describes further on in his essay (see below).[113] This acausal principle of connection i.e., resemblance of form, thus applies even when more impressive or "numinous" reactions occur in the subject, as reported in this article from *Time* magazine:

> On the very afternoon that Jung died in Zurich, writes van der Post, "lightning struck his favorite tree in the garden." Van der Post was on a ship bound from Africa at the time. Unaware that his old friend had died, he had a vision of Jung atop the Matterhorn. He was waving and calling out, "I'll be seeing you." Some years later, van der Post was filming a documentary at the Jung house in Zurich. "When the moment came for me to speak directly to the camera about Jung's death," he recalls, "and I came to the description of how lightning demolished Jung's favorite tree, the lightning struck in the garden again."[114]

As I said earlier, Jung's understanding of synchronicity may be expressed as the acausal principle of resemblance of forms. This principle therefore suggests that the relevant psychological question to ask of synchronicity concerns the *living* connection between the images of the events comprising the synchronicity, i.e., how do the forms or images resemble one another? To answer such questions of resemblance or similarity we must appeal to the imagination since *only* the imagination can *perceive* resemblances as *alive* and meaningfully connected, as Jung clearly shows above. The modern mind, 5 being largely devoid of the imagination today in its apprehension of appearances, can scarcely grasp Page of 3 8how our forbears, without being the least troubled, could for example perceive a clear *living* resemblance between the mineral gold, various plants and herbs, the human heart, the lion, the sun, a constellation of stars (Leo), royalty, and divinity. The medieval mind, still imbued with the faculty of the imagination could easily perceive how all these *living* appearances resemble one another. The medieval mind could also *think* the objective implicit meaning binding these resemblances—in this case the highest value for them—God!

In our modern times, reports of a lightning strike occurring simultaneously with Jung's death and with van der Post's dream must remain, at best, a description of an unusual, and impressive temporal co-incidence of otherwise unrelated empirical events. The modern mind only understands cause-effect connections which are ontologically "dead". They do not "speak" to us. But once these random events are spoken into ordinary language, i.e., become linguistic experiences, the speaker or reader begins to psychologically participate (this being the nature of language) in the experience. Now the imagination and only the imagination can begin to perceive *living* connections between these otherwise random events. For example, Jung's psyche had gathered a series of remembered, previously disconnected empirical events over 24 hours *via* the principle of resemblance. He then wrote out all these now *linguistic* acausal meaningful connections from memory. From the nest of linguistic resemblances we can now see a central meaning emerge from Jung's participation with the images—the symbol of the fish! The various resemblances that he had perceived sequentially outwardly over twenty-four hours, when gathered together by Jung's psyche, constituted a representation of an implicit meaning pressing forward into consciousness in Jung the perceiver as the symbol of the fish.

A series of empirically unconnected random events subsequently *became* acausally connected through Jung's spontaneous imaginative efforts to bring the "run of events" into language by his writing out the passage I am referring to. This "run of events" now became a linguistic experience of synchronicity. Jung was impressed by this experience to the point that he called the phenomenon "numinous". However, he declined the temptation of regarding numinosity as an explanatory principle for synchronicity.[115] He simply said:

> We should then have to *assume* (my italics) that events in general are related to one another on the one hand as causal changes, and on the other hand by a kind of meaningful cross connection. [116]

I have not seen any other modern attempt to offer an explanation for synchronicity that explores the difference between events as perceived by modern empirical consciousness (devoid of the imagination) and thus connected only causally if at all and events that *become* a linguistic experience through the act of writing or some other art form. This creative act of writing engages the imagination and its principle of resemblance of form.

Let's now explore this proposal in the example from Time magazine (see above).

At first, when we read the report of a lightning strike, Jung's death, van der Post's dream, and his subsequent filming some years later, we perceive a "dead letter," i.e., a document that holds only surface literal meaning, describing a random co-incidence of empirical events. I want now to invoke the wisdom of a visionary artist—Kandinsky.

> Everything that is dead quivers. Not only the things of poetry, stars, moon, wood, flowers, but even a white trouser button glittering out of a puddle in the street...Everything has a secret soul, which is silent more often than it speaks.

Kandinsky knows that just below the surface of our modern empirical lives a different order of quivering *life* prevails—that of the imagination or in more modern terms the objective psyche. This largely forgotten *organ of perception*, can, as Kandinsky knows, perceive *living* (quivering) resemblances between empirically unconnected images, gathering them together in a way that suggest an implicit meaning in which the artist (his unconscious) participates.

Having read the Time report, I'll begin by asking psyche for resemblances between lightning strikes, Jung's death, van der Post's dream, and his subsequent filming some years later. I immediately receive a response—"intuition". There can be no doubt about Jung's intuitive capacity. There is much documentation on record of his amazing healing abilities involving intuition. So, flashes of lightning resemble flashes of intuition. Van der Post's dream at the time of Jung's death points to a similar intuitive capacity in van der Post. His psyche sensed Jung's death in the image of his own dream at the time. The second occasion also links intuition with Jung with the added twist of van der Post's *speaking* of Jung's death when lightning strikes again.

As I write this out I begin to sense an implicit meaning emerging from the nest of resemblances. Lightning strikes, intuition, Jung, and significantly, Jung's death; also van der Post speaking of Jung's death. I now remember Jung's image in van der Post's dream cheerily exclaiming "I'll be seeing you!" This image releases a stream of further questions in me, all intuitively directed towards the unknown future: what is van der Post intuiting here, *via* his dream? Or could it be that a prophecy is being made and that the addressee may be not only van der Post but perhaps *us*, their future generations?

With this discovery of implicit meaning arising from van der Post's synchronicity, I felt a rising enthusiasm. As with any prophecy, meaning is veiled as much as unconcealed—is Jung inviting us over to the other side in a Shivaic gesture of "don't be afraid"? Or is the prophecy suggesting that he may come again Christ-like in some other form? Or is the intuition pointing to a coming time when the locus of subjectivity moves from the ego as subject to the *other* as subject—*I'll* be seeing *you*"—meaning that in the future we may experience ourselves as being perceived by a greater *other*?

My purpose here is to demonstrate a method of addressing synchronicities that relies on the principle of resemblances applied to acausal connections found in the act of bringing otherwise discreet, random empirical events into language in which psyche is reflecting itself today. Note that this method has no need to refer to the ontological status of any one event, e.g. *via* the inner/outer distinction. The canonical interpretation of synchronicity depends on making this distinction and then maintaining it methodologically while wrestling with the self-induced conundrum of how "inner" and "outer" *can* be "one" (the *unus mundus*). This imaginative method also needs no explanatory principle such as "numinous experience", an explanatory principle for synchronicity that Jung also eschews.

I'll leave my excursion into the theory of synchronicity here and return, more adequately equipped, to our clinical session. We are now re-entering the linguistic world of another synchronicity I described as the Night of the Rat.

THE NECESSARY SACRIFICE OF THE RAT

As I said, the couple believed the rat's death had no significance for their nearly terminal marriage. For them the sequence of temporal events was simply randomly empirical. For the couple, the telling of the story of the Night of the Rat was a dead letter! In contrast I felt something quivering beneath the surface of their story. My imagination had apparently quivered in recognition of some resemblances in Page of 5 8the story that were, so far, veiled from my understanding and, of course, that of my clients. And so I waited.

When I finally spoke, I was working rat-like "in the dark". I asked each participant in turn to tell us what kind of being human *could* be like a rat. I was seeking resemblances between the images of their story. One can only answer that question if the *life* of the imagination is available to them. The betrayed partner began by recalling habitual associations of human and rat—people who "rat" on each other; "rats" who live in places of dark secrets and seediness; money dealings whose currency is deceit, betrayal, exploitation, etc. As she spoke I did not feel much imaginative *life* in these associations. They were as I said routine habits of thought, easily retrievable through memory.

I then turned to her partner and his story of the events that night. To our collective shock he began to reveal implicit aspects of the "dead letter" that he had completely omitted in the first telling. He told us he had been appalled by the sight of an innocent creature struggling in its death-throes, its brains spilling over the floor. This was an innocent creature, he said, which had died so horribly by his hand— he had laid the trap that previous day and he was the cause of its agony and death.

The most compelling aspect to this now very *alive* imaginative account of the event was the shift in the man's attitude. His *mea culpa* had completely gone. In all his previous attempts to connect with his wife's agony in the face of his multiple betrayals, deceptions and "mind-fucking" over many years, his subjectivity had remained at the centre: "I am so sorry about what I have done to you. How can I help you to make ME feel better, to remove MY guilt and shame, so that we can move on past the suffering as quickly as possible." This self-serving and exclusive focus on the subject whenever we addressed his wife's agonies had seemed intractable to me.

Until now!

All traces of a wilful subject suddenly disappeared and the objective suffering of the "innocent" rat that was "only trying to survive" was now in focus! The husband, perhaps for the first time in his adult life, was feeling *compassion* for the victim. He could now sense an implicit identity with the rat through the *living* resemblance between the form of the rat's fate and that of his own. *His* brains had been dashed out and he could now feel the agony of his heart.

None of us had any preconceived idea that his wife's suffering, the rat's agony and indeed his own pain were associated by resemblances linked by the hidden yet quivering meaning of a *necessary sacrifice* of innocence giving rise to true compassion.

The man's psyche had "arranged" those fateful events that evening (he had set the trap) in order to bring forth that meaning of a necessary sacrifice of innocence—a meaning that shocked us all. He and his wife had lived lives of "innocence"—never thinking beyond surface matters of self-serving comfort, making money and not asking questions about life beyond seeking material ends. Neither had any concern about the possibility of sudden violent incursions from the *depths* of our human being that might disturb their complacent style of surface living—that is, until such an incursion happened!

His secret life of empty sex, deceit, and evasiveness, had been successfully hidden from his wife, family, community—*and himself.* They were shocked into the soul *depths* of life, never to return to their former lives of "innocent" survival. They now know very dark aspects of each other's being, previously hidden from their conscious awareness of what life is about. There is no return to that innocence.

WORKING WITH SYNCHRONICITY

The story or narrative of the synchronistic events of that fateful night was at first a "dead letter". Then a quivering started up from below the surface of the narrative. Perhaps I felt it first. I began the inner work of bringing language to those quivers or tremblings—to offer myself as a mouthpiece for the silent *depths* lying "within" the dead letter of the story. Most importantly, I had no interest in any division between "inner" and "outer" or in any "numinous" aspect to the story. In their telling us the story of that night, my only concern was with giving the the images constituting the story a "voice", based on the imagination's capacity to perceive *living* resemblances.

Privileging the image is a sharp methodological contrast to the usual ontological approach to synchronicity, i.e., asking whether an event is psychic or empirical, for example, and whether their simultaneous appearance, along with our subjective emotions or reactions to the synchronicity demonstrate an underlying unitary reality—*unus mundus* or "one world".

As soon as we "speak" or otherwise *ensoul* an empirical event we begin to engage one another from within our shared linguistic world. The logical structure of our shared linguistic world, i.e., the world 10 we call ordinary or quotidian is such that what we perceive "out there" has an veiled *interiority* that is also in some sense *our* interiority. What we perceive "out there" is also an unconscious representation of *us*! This is the husband's discovery in the telling of the Night of the Rat when he entered the image of the slaughtered, innocent rat by speaking it and suddenly feeling its agony as his own.

His participation became conscious. We discovered an implicit meaning in the narrative of the synchronicity—one that also has something to do with us, namely, a *necessary* bloody sacrifice of psychological "innocence" keeping us on the surface of unconscious life, merely surviving (as he said of the rat) while remaining oblivious to any other dimension of the human experience.

Once that meaning was made explicit through speech, I suggested to the husband that this sudden opening to compassion may give him the eyes to similarly view his wife's suffering. Compassion has nothing to do with him as subject or his personal difficulties in taking responsibility for his actions. Instead the eyes of compassion have everything to do with the suffering of the *other*, even the *other* in himself that he had hitherto ignored completely, until his soul "arranged" the perfect synchronicity to bring his psychological innocence to a sacrificial end.

ADDENDUM.

1. Whatever one may think about Rudolph Steiner's cosmology, throughout his work he gives ample examples of the imagination's capacity to perceive real resemblances of form in the world, across scale: One can actually say: just as man carries around in his intestines the products of his digestion, so does the cosmos carry around—indirectly by way of the earth— the toads, snakes, and frogs in the cosmic intestine which it formed in the watery-earthly element of the Earth. It is with the same forces by means of which man digests, that the outer cosmos, outer nature, forms

snakes, toads, lizards and frogs…The mineral kingdom is the deposit of the plant and animal-kingdom, and it is actually the deposit of the lowest animals. The toads do not contribute very much to the mineral element of the earth; the fishes, too, comparatively little; but the lower animals and the plants contribute a very great deal.

And note: he has successfully introduced many cultural practices based on this capacity of the imagination.[117]

2. In 2012, I wrote a book of essays that describe a series of synchronicities over several years in the nineties.[118]

PART TWO

Any cultural production can be viewed solely in terms of the consciousness of exteriority (subject-object)—the structure of consciousness that is rooted in the inner/outer, or subject/object binaries. When viewed in this typical manner, artistic or cultural forms remain simply objects "over there", silent, entertaining, and making no claim on (the being of) the viewer.

The following essays are the result of an anomaly: a sudden penetration that breaks down these habitual binaries, giving me a glimpse of future appearances, and making a claim on me. As I leave the theatre, close the book, or wake up from a dream, sometimes I am left with a resonating feeling. After several decades of familiarity with this feeling I know that something is about to speak and that I must be silent as possible in order to "hear" and participate in its speaking.

A VATAR: LOST DREAMS OR MODERN NIGHTMARE

To concern ourselves with dreams is a way of reflecting on ourselves—a way of self reflection. It is not our ego-consciousness reflecting itself ... It reflects not on the ego ... but recollects that strange self, alien to the ego.

C. G. Jung

OK, so now we know that all box office records are broken, once again, and our fascination with extreme ends of the scales is sated once more: "the biggest ... grossing the most ... technical wonder ...".[119] We also can read the professional reviews to get criticism of the art form itself. In reading or hearing reviews from the audiences, there can be no doubt that the world of Pandora is a very compelling world indeed, enough for some to consider suicide after seeing the movie:

> When I woke up this morning after watching Avatar for the first time yesterday, the world seemed grey. It was like my whole life, everything I've done and worked for, lost its meaning ... It just seems so meaningless. I still don't really see any reason to keep doing things at all. I live in a dying world.[120]

Many reviews seem to me to circle around "hype" or the "thrill" or the captivating qualities of Pandora but what kind of world is being represented here? Every review I have read points to a lost world of our past, a nostalgic longing for a natural world saturated with meaning and interconnectedness. This interpretation is probably what is behind the suicidal sentiments expressed above. It is hard to bear the loss of meaning and profound isolation we are living today.

Equally, no review I have read gives a mention of the central symbol of the movie. The central symbol is not Pandora which, as a symbol, has indeed gripped us hard. The central symbol in the movie lies in the title: Avatar! In my own research of the effects of this movie on the audience, nobody I talked to mentioned the word Avatar in terms of its symbolism! What's even more incredible to me is that nobody I talked to knew what "Avatar" means in the modern context. This omission of any discussion of the most obvious and central symbol in the movie constitutes the anomaly that struck me forcibly, and released this essay.

So, what is an avatar today?

While I am writing this review, tens of millions of people are online, doing what the movie represents so well, in so much detail, and with an astonishing acceptance of its ordinariness. The fact that millions on a daily basis are already doing what the movie dramatizes may account for this easy acceptance of the movie's premise and central symbol. Millions, maybe tens of millions now are entering their own avatar in order to inhabit another world for as long as they like. If you have not yet heard of this phenomenon, take a look at: www.secondlife.com. If you want to explore the seamier side of this phenomenon, just type in "virtual sex". You will be astonished at the science that is supporting the invention of mechanisms designed to convince the user of the sensual qualities of the reality they have entered as their avatar.

This is not a movie about a lost innocence. It is training manual for the West, urging us to go further in what we can already do, in the millions: enter virtual reality as an avatar and go into, not nature, but cyberspace, or virtual reality. Avatar is the common name known to millions of "gamers" who daily enter their digitalized version of "Pandora" and engage in the same impossible feats that are shown in the movie. The beautiful images of Pandora, which have no correspondence at all with empirical nature on earth, are merely the technological means (graphics, 3-D, CGI, etc.) by which the modern ego is captivated and seduced into leaving earthly reality and entering virtual reality, perhaps forever, as our hero did. But note well, when he did succeed finally in becoming a Pandorian resident, his earthly body died!

This is no mere fantasy. Millions are doing it already. This movie simply acts as an openly seductive engine designed to encourage a particular "solution" to our loss of meaning and isolation. Our collective nostalgia for the past, a fancied innocence and primordial oneness etc. is simply the "unconscious desire" that can be caught and manipulated towards other ends, as the public relations industry knows so well. For all those who think it is about primordial nature and rediscovering our interconnectedness, I would urge them to remember how our hero enters Pandora: he lies in a coffin and "dies", just as millions do when they log on. They die to the ordinary world and their bodies waste away as they spend 12 or 16 hours online in cyberspace enjoying their freedom! Yes, freedom, real freedom! Freedom from ordinary reality which is becoming harder to bear as we witness the accelerating emptying out of meaning in the natural world!

Avatar is a movie that encourages what millions really want to do, spelling out the method to enter cyberspace, at the cost of earthly life altogether. Avatar is decidedly not a movie urging us to reclaim our interconnectedness and oneness with nature. Pandora is not a representation of nature at all. It is a true and accurate representation of what we are already building and investing billions of dollars in: cyberspace or virtual reality, which is a reality indeed but not a natural one.

When our unconscious desires, e.g. nostalgia for a fancied past, are excited and aroused with captivating and well chosen images, we lose our discerning minds and thus confound a yearning for a "lost dream" with the denial of a living modern nightmare that is emerging before our occluded eyes. The entire engine of our modern technological society is now geared towards the development of cyberspace into which we are now openly being invited. We are to inhabit it in exactly the way shown by the movie, leaving behind, as the movie also shows, dead bodies, and a dead Earth.

THE GIRL WITH THE DRAGON TATTOO:
End of Hope, Initiation of Consciousness

Patrick Henry (1736-1799), one of the Founding Fathers of the USA once said:

> It is natural for man to indulge in the illusions of hope. We are apt to shut our eyes against a painful truth, and listen to the song of that siren till she transforms us into beasts ... For my part, whatever anguish of spirit it may cost, I am willing to know the whole truth, to know the worst, and to provide for it.

In this essay I want to take this thought further. What painful truth does hope blind us to, and what will it take to bring hope to an end and so open our eyes to this painful truth?

A movie, The Girl with the Dragon Tattoo, came out recently and shows in unsparing detail what that painful truth is and what kind of initiation will bring an end to hope and open us up sufficiently to be transformed by that truth.[121] First, let's hear the dialogue that is crucial to my argument here. The journalist, Mikael Blomkvist (MB) is captured by serial killer Martin Vanger (MV) who takes him to a soundproof cellar with the intent to hang the journalist:

> **MV:** Scream as much as you can. Do you think anyone can hear you? We both know how it is going to end for you.

> **MB:** Why?

> **MV:** Why what?

> **MB:** All of this (i.e., the apparatus, the murders, rapes, tortures . . .)

> **MV:** Why not? I'm doing what every man dreams of. I take what I want.

> **MB:** How many women after the first?

MV: I don't know. I have lost count. I had a girl in that cage when we were dining upstairs. Those kinds of women disappear all the time. Nobody misses them. Whores. Immigrants.

MB: What do you do with them? What about the references (to race, religion), the mutilations?

(MV places a noose around MB's neck, loosely.)

MV: That was my father's project. He mixed his hobby with race and religion. But it was a mistake. You shouldn't leave the bodies behind. I take them for a trip in my boat and I drop them into the sea. Marie was my first.

MB: '64. You were sixteen

MV: It was Dad, Gottfried, who taught me how to strangle her.

MB: It's sick.

MV: It's mainly for the sex. When I put them down its only a logical consequence of the rape. You can't leave any witnesses. Even though I have to admit. I love seeing their disappointment.

MB: Disappointment?

MV: When they realize they'll die. It doesn't really fit into their scheme of things. They always think I'll show them mercy. It's a fantastic moment when they realize they are not getting away. When their eyes switch off and die. You'll experience that yourself.

MB: And your sister? What did it feel like when your sister's eyes died?

MV: Harriett disappeared.

MB: You want me to believe that.

MV: Believe what the hell you want to. I would have enjoyed killing her but she disappeared. Just like you'll disappear. Do you want some water?

MB: Yes please … Thanks.

(MV gently gives him a sip of water.)

MV: You see, you're just like everybody else. It only takes a simple human gesture to ignite the small hope that I might let you go after all. Right? (pulls the noose tight). Take it easy. It'll be quick.

This is a gruelling scene but one that is quite illuminating in regards to the process of ending hope and opening the eyes to a painful truth. So let's "unpack" the dialogue a bit.

Martin Vanger is a serial killer in the plot but as a figure of the artistic imagination, expressing a truth about our times he is much more. He refers to his grisly deeds as a *hobby* in which he can take what he wants, i.e. satisfy every possible dark desire, without consequence. He is thus an ultimate figure of *leisure time*, time in which no responsibility exists.

This time is a recent invention and is now institutionalised, supported with billions of dollars across the world: entertainment, tourism, mass sporting events, Internet games and virtual reality, etc. Vanger, as an ultimate symbol of this time has successfully escaped the bonds of necessity in existence. He maintains his status as a free-floating consciousness by making sure there are no witnesses to his cruelty. He kills and carefully disposes of the dead bodies. As he says it is purely a matter of logic. In this way he separates deed from consequence, in accord with the logical structure of leisure or "free" time today.

On the human level, Vanger is a sadist, torturer, and murderer and he sets about bringing an end to Blomkvist's life the same way as his other victims, but the richness and complexity of the sparse dialogue reveals much more going on than the human level. We are being shown what an unmitigated attack on hope looks like and from what quarter it will come.

Vanger relentlessly tells Blomqvist how each victim, in spite of his sadistic sexual attacks, still holds out a morsel of hope that he will release them. He gets a special delight in watching the disappointment as the knowledge, yes *knowledge*, finally dawns that there is no way out, no escape! The victims are literally bound by ropes but the more fundamental bindings are those of the logic of their situation ("no witnesses") which becomes obvious when hope is finally abandoned.

Vanger sets about delivering the same message to Blomqvist. He first arouses hope by offering a small glass of water, almost tenderly, without malice and then, when Blomqvist is refreshed, he delivers the enlightening teaching, "You see, you're just like everybody else. It only takes a simple human gesture to ignite the small hope that I might let you go after all. Right?" Vanger then tightens the noose and leaves Blomqvist to suffocate, "take it easy. It'll be quick."

Although this is a scene of "no exit", in the film a rescue occurs at the hands of the girl and the evil one is dispatched. The girl herself is a very interesting figure of the imagination too. In our collective desire to be "free", i.e. to be absolved from the necessities of existence, we tend to praise this figure. She is the hacker who can do anything, including making herself very rich and exacting cruel acts of revenge on her tormentors. She is an embodiment of that very freedom that we and indeed the serial killer seek. We forget that she too is a monster—remember the scene in which she douses her father, yes violent father, and lights him up like a candle? She also freely torments her sadistic probation officer, employing a rather malicious imagination herself, making sure logistically, as does the serial killer, that she avoids any consequences of her own incredibly cruel actions. She also lives without hope and teaches the probation officer to do the same, binding him to necessity, carving her justice into his body, just as the serial killer does to his victims.

Both the girl and the serial killer are therefore alternate figures of that structure of consciousness that lives in leisure time, time that is absolved of responsibilities, or the necessities that come inevitably with existence. It does no good to praise one and condemn the other!

As I watched this compelling movie, I suddenly apperceived it as an artistic rendering of an initiatory process for the modern mind. How can these figures be images of an initiatory process?

Again, turning to the movie, we can see how the girl carves "I am a rapist" into the chest of the probation officer. He finally got it! Something got through to him as objective knowledge! Vanger too impresses upon his victims the futility of hope. Disappointment is followed by a dawning knowledge, knowledge that there is *no way out*. Hope won't do it. Hope won't get through because our "free" egos are now pretty well insulated from life.

We live in leisure time within which as I said we choose "freely" i.e., without consequence, because this freedom is only an abstraction, having the same logical status as wishful thinking. But initiation *does* get through! Initiation is a process in which a subject other than the ego gets through, makes an impression, leaves a scar for life (this is the meaning of the scarification rituals of the past), and transforms consciousness.

It seems to me that this movie is a vehicle for expressing a background movement in which the "free" modern ego can be initiated into the *truth* of the present structure of consciousness-world in which deed is *logically* separated and dissociated from consequence. While we dissociate deed from consequence, we generate, for the first time in history, leisure time, within which we can "rule the universe". The serial killer is merely a fictional figure portraying what the "free" ego does every day—video games, entertainment, leisure pursuits, internet activities, holidays, in which we behave in ways we could not possibly do at home. Outside this leisure time, we remain *objectively* ruled and dominated by the economy, employment, illnesses, fragmented relationships etc.

Our freedoms and our necessities are dissociated from each other.

This structure of consciousness will work its will upon us until all hope is gone and its reality becomes our truth (it *is* and we *know* it to be so!). This will happen as we are attacked or penetrated by the very logic of the "free" ego that we are today. What we *are* must first appear to us as an *other*, impervious to hope and beyond emotion, human feeling etc. ruled only by its own logic. At first, disappointment, followed by a dawning knowledge, inaugurating the "death" of that structure of consciousness as it fulfills its moment. What is this dawning knowledge?

When we are assailed by the underlying logical structure of "free" ego, i.e. as *other*, constituted as a dissociation between deed and consequence, or freedom and necessity, with all hope gone, it will begin to dawn on us that such freedom in fact carries its own necessity, and its deeds contain their own consequences and have done so all along. Our "free" leisure time will inevitably be seen to be a prison of necessity and our free leisure pursuits will be seen to be consequential after all. It will become obvious that we have not really escaped necessity or the consequences of our freedom at all. When this realization comes home, the "free" ego will die and another structure of consciousness will emerge, but best not to get ahead of ourselves here ...

THE BIG SHORT

The Big Short (2016) springs from the acclaimed book of the same name by Michael Lewis (2011), which tells the story of the 2008 financial crash from the points of view of those very few traders who could see it coming and decided to bet against (short) the "certainty" that there would be no such crash.[122] As you could imagine, Wall Street had no hesitation in taking their money ("free money," as one character said, working for Goldman Sachs at the time) and soon these intrepid investors were paying millions of dollars in premiums to the gleeful investment banks, while the years rolled by, getting closer and closer to 2007. Then, when the cracks in the financial system began to show and the value of the "insured" financial entities began to fall to zero, Wall Street had to pay out, in turn, to the traders who reaped the rewards of their risks to the tune of hundreds of millions of dollars, while the financial system of the USA finally had to get bailed out by the US taxpayer in the amounts of trillions of dollars.

You will have to read the book and see the movie to even begin to understand how it all works and even then, you won't. No one knows. It's too complicated. That's why no one except for a man with Asperger's, along a few others, could see it coming. So I will not be giving you another layman's inadequate version of the central financial features that brought the system down: NINJAs, subprime loans, CDO's, CD swaps, tranches, etc. The movie did an excellent job at that, as did Lewis in his book.

My task here is different. I will not try to understand

the text or script in the usual way of subject-centered interpretations applying familiar categories of understanding.[123] Instead, I found myself participating in what has been called a hermeneutic reversal, in which a meaning implicit in the text became alive, as a subject, and appropriated my understanding to its *telos* of manifestation. To give you a taste of how a text can serve living meaning in this way, I will tell the story of Jason Elliot in Afghanistan when he visited a shrine, a tomb of Sufi saint.

> What appeared from a distance to be the shading within these shapes was in fact a mosaic of angularly stylized Arabic characters, with each character itself composed of tinier tiles. ... the mosaics themselves depicted verses from the Qur'an ... Something was getting under my skin as my eyes roamed the walls. I had a feeling that this was different from any art I had ever seen. And in that cold, lowering dusk, in that shabby courtyard, where the tile work is a third destroyed, a ray of meaning seemed to leap from the walls. It was as if they had suddenly become articulate and, shedding for a moment their almost formal precision, began to dance and weave with meaning. ... This was not the art of decoration but of sacred ciphers, in which the onlooker is invited to participate, not merely stand in awe, and decode the patterns according to his means.[124]

As I struggled with The Big Short, through the tortured and convoluted financial dealings of the trading world, tripping over the endless acronyms that the bond market invented to obscure its shady bets, a meaning "leaped from the pages," as Elliott describes. And this is what I want to tell you about. To do so, unfortunately, I have to make an attempt to briefly talk about the financial entity that lies at the bottom of the 2008 catastrophe—a catastrophe that Lewis describes this way:

> On Wall Street in 2008 the reality finally overwhelmed perceptions: A crowded theater burned down with a lot of people still in their seats. Every major firm on Wall Street was either bankrupt or fatally intertwined with a bankrupt system. ... the International Monetary Fund would put losses on U.S.-originated subprime-related assets at a trillion dollars. One trillion dollars in losses had been created by American financiers, out of whole cloth, and embedded in the American financial system. Each Wall Street firm held some share of those losses, and could do nothing to avoid them. No Wall Street firm would be able to extricate itself, as there were no longer any buyers. It was as if bombs of differing sizes had been placed in virtually every major Western financial institution. The fuses had been lit and could not be extinguished. All that remained was to observe the speed of the spark, and the size of the explosions.

This catastrophe was also called the subprime crisis. Here is my layman's description. I know a little about it because I was one of the consumers who took out a subprime mortgage loan back in 2001. These loans were typically made to people whose financial status normally disbarred them from owning a home (NINJA —no income, no job). In fact the lenders did not want them to repay the loan. They were drawn in by teaser interest rates (that went up in two years to 12.5%), and told they did not have to make any payments but to simply roll the owed interest payments into an accruing principal balance. This would last for two years until the interest rate jumped and there was no hope of repayments. And so, as a result, the defaults on the loans began to avalanche.

But why did the lenders make such risky loans in the first place? This remarkable lack of restraint in lending has to do with what the lenders did with the loans, once acquired. They sold them to firms such as Goldman Sachs who packaged huge numbers of such almost valueless loans into bonds (CDO's), with various credit ratings attached to them, that could then be sold to investors.[125] With this financial instrument in place, the original real-life debts owned by real people became represented as a financial asset which could be further manipulated by the money market, in essence functioning in a very sophisticated betting ring, as the movie demonstrates so well.

More instruments (such as CD swaps) were invented to even further distance the financial world from the empirical reality of the growing number of defaulting mortgagees. The ever-increasing abstractions reached such a level of sophistication and complexity that, when the bubble finally burst, no financial expert knew what had happened. The US government even turned to the author Michael Lewis for help:

> The story was also "serious," in the sense that important people felt they needed to know about it. The instant the book was published it brought with it another experience new to me, the interest of politicians. In the space of a few months I was asked to address one large room filled with Republican

Congressmen, and another large room filled with Democratic Congressmen. ... But Wall Street had grown so complicated that it was virtually impossible for an outsider to understand it without help. After an ordinary financial crisis political leaders typically would turn to the people on Wall Street whom they trusted, for advice and education. After this financial crisis there was no one on Wall Street whom they could trust. The sort of people who had once formed the American financial elite had so discredited themselves that United States Senators no longer believed they were capable of giving honest advice to their country in its time of need. And so the Senators began to read up on the subject for themselves.

As I waded through this financial miasma with the help of author Michael Lewis, the meaning I referred to earlier began to leap out at me, and it is simply this: the entire financial world, the world of money and its machinations, is simply a reflection of a far deeper process that is manifesting in many other walks of life today. It has to do with representational reality!

I will explain.

First, actual people who could not possibly afford to repay any loan were enticed into buying a home (in one case, the movie shows a stripper owning five apartments under this scheme). When subprime loans are bundled together and named as CDOs (collateralized debt obligation), the "reality" status of the original empirical situation undergoes a transformation. Where we had real people buying homes, we now have a subprime loan, i.e. documentation that *represents* the real situation. When millions of these loans are packaged into bonds then these posited bonds now represent millions of loans whose "individuality" gets completely lost. There was no way for anyone to investigate the status of individual loans that were wrapped up in the CDOs, and therefore it was impossible to rate their financial credit status:

> "… the scary thing was, my managers didn't know anything either. I asked these basic questions—like, Why do they own this mortgage bond? Are they just betting on it or is it some part of a larger strategy?" … there was effectively no way for an accountant assigned to audit a giant Wall Street firm to figure out whether it was making money or losing money. They were giant black boxes, whose hidden gears were in constant motion.[126]

The representational nature of mortgage loans (the documentation) and then the bonds (representing the bundled documentations) was lost and a new financial (virtual) reality was posited. These instruments became entities that had a 'life' of their own and were treated as having a "thing" nature, no longer understood as representational. This capacity to *posit* reality belongs to a subject centered consciousness which posits meaning on an otherwise lifeless world:

> Where the world becomes picture, beings as a whole are set in place as that for which man is prepared; that which, therefore, he correspondingly intends to bring before him, and, nearby, in a decisive sense, place before him. A being is first and only in being is so far as it is set in place by representing-producing humanity.[127]

Heidegger is pointing to our modern structure of

consciousness in which the human being has become the subject and for whom the world has become a picture for us and only has being *as that picture*. The picture's representational character is lost to us. Any aspect of being that cannot be represented scientifically (measured, objectified) simply disappears into oblivion as far as the constructed world picture and its corresponding cultural practices are concerned. This world picture now *is* the new reality and the financial system is simply one cultural form that arose accordingly. With an increasingly complex array of financial instruments, Wall Street replaced one representation (which had already lost its reference to anything real on the empirical level) with another and proceeded to relate to that representation literally, lifting off empirical reality altogether into the stratosphere of what shall we call it, purely fictional or virtual reality (but not understood as such)?

The underlying meaning of the Crash is this: The global financial system is a cultural form rooted in the human being as subject who *posits* reality (generating a world *picture*). This definition of the human being shows that all meaning must come from this subject and be imposed on an otherwise silent and meaningless world. "Descartes" is the symbol that conveys this form of consciousness in much of the literature today but the historical roots that produced the meaning-bearing human subject go deeper than the 16th century.

What happens to human beings who blindly or habitually enact this form of **consciousness?** Lewis' book is replete with examples of the human wreckage that is the consequence of such blindness. First and foremost we see that abstracting from ordinary reality and privileging that abstraction *as* reality, blinds human beings to theirs and others' humanity.

For example, lets talk about Michael Burry. He is the hero of Lewis' book, a fund manager suffering from Asperger's Syndrome, who shunned human companionship. His syndrome enabled him to do what no other trader wanted to do: study the mind-numbing prospectuses of hundreds of mortgage bonds. In so doing his eyes were opened to the fictitious nature of the bonds—they were backed by loans that had no real value (the NINJAs who could not possibly pay the interest on their mortgages). He proceeded to short these bonds (bet against any increase in their value) and in few years made a profit of $750 million for the investors in his fund. You'd think they would be grateful! Here is what happened to Burry at the end of it all:

> In 2007 alone Burry had made his investors $750 million—and yet now he had only $600 million under management. His investors' requests for their money back came in hard and fast. No new investors called— not a single one. Nobody called him to solicit his views of the world, or his predictions for the future, either. So far as he could see, no one even seemed to want to know how he had done what he had done.[128]

On October 27, Burry wrote to one of his two e-mail friends: "I'm selling off the positions tonight. I think I hit a breaking point. I haven't eaten today, I'm not sleeping, I'm not talking with my kids, not talking with my wife, I'm broken. Asperger's has given me some great gifts, but life's been too hard for too long because of it as well." On a Friday afternoon in early November, he felt chest pains and went to an emergency room. His blood pressure had spiked. "I felt like I am heading towards a short life," he wrote. A week later, on November 12, he sent his final letter to investors. "I have been pushed repeatedly to the brink by my own actions, the Fund's investors, business partners, and even former employees," he wrote. "I have always been able to pull back and carry on my often overly intense affair with this business. Now, however, I am facing personal matters that have carried me irrefutably over the threshold, and I have come to the sullen realization that I must close down the Fund." With that, he vanished, leaving a lot of people wondering what had happened.[129]

The movie is filled with similar examples of people treating one another badly—very badly. It seems that when a world is posited and a world picture generated, which is then treated as reality with its entities having a "thing" status, human beings, along with bonds, are treated merely as part of that increasingly abstract (virtual) reality. The human-ness of human beings drops off into oblivion because our humanity cannot be measured or represented, or abstracted, without losing its essence. Burry goes on to say something remarkable: "The thing is, I haven't identified what it [the business] kills. But it is something vital that is dead inside of me. I can feel it."[130]

The financial system, as a cultural form (maybe the dominant one now), displays the underlying structure of consciousness-world that gives rise to such forms (what I call here the underlying *meaning*) in the first place. Elsewhere I show that this determining structure has already undergone another transformation, with the consequence that the present stabilized forms of culture are no longer expressive of the new underlying logical structure but instead are maintained through habit only. The financial Crash is expressive of the fact that such cultural forms are no longer supported by the objective psyche (the determining logic or structure of any cultural form) and so must be supported only by habit, human willfulness, and terror. To use a financial term, the human *cost*, in maintaining a cultural form that Life (the logic of Life) has now left behind, is devastating.[131]

We are now acting against Life and its transformational movements and the moneymen are showing us the human cost. Neither winners nor losers are spared. Interestingly, the cost invariably lies in experiences of our embodied being, that aspect of Life that has nothing to do with any world picture and so is consigned to oblivion. My book, Oblivion of Being, goes into this question and points the way to a new structure of consciousness and its correspondingly new cultural forms. In this book I ask:

> A new birth on Earth—now the true world ...   is bestowed on us as "already happened and unnoticed in language." But how is this new true world configured? What are its contours? And what kind of human being is able to perceive these contours? How can it be *spoken*?[132]

BIRDMAN:
The Unexpected Virtue Of Ignorance

"Koyaanisqatsi" is a Hopi word, translated as "life out of balance". The 1982 movie of the same name portrays Western civilization caught in an accelerating trajectory towards disaster. The last scene captures the movie's intention with an image of utter self-destruction. A space-bound rocket—the epitome of American ambition and pride—explodes in a fireball and then plunges, tumbling in slow motion, along a flaming arc back to earth accompanied by the poignant, insistent music of Philip Glass.

Birdman surprisingly opens up with a similar image.[133] We see a large incandescent body slowly careening across the New York sky for long moments—the first appearance of an anomaly breaking in to our ordinary world. At first it looks like a comet, which is portentous enough, but then the flames suggest a huge meteor entering the atmosphere, or even a version of the 2003 Columbia disaster. It, too, does not bode well!

The plot then takes us deep inside the world of acting and the two major art forms of the USA: movies and theatre. There is even a "play within a play" structure reminiscent of Hamlet, in which both plays mirror each other's theme. In Hamlet the inner play shows the Prince what he must do—a rehearsal for a necessary decision in life! But when he encounters a similar situation for real, as a participant within the larger play, his courage fails him. Although the protagonist in the inner play finally acts decisively (Pyrrhus slaying Priam), Hamlet cannot transport that knowledge of what he must do into action. This dramatic structure is analogous to that of a dream "within" waking life. The dreamer is portrayed as a player in a drama, and yet, upon waking, the dreamer is often unable to convey any of the dream's truth into relevant action in life. The dream, or in Hamlet's case, the inner play, could not *penetrate* the dreamer's (or Hamlet's) waking consciousness enough to affect his course of action or inaction in life.

The inner play of Birdman is a dramatized version of Raymond Carver's short story, "What We Talk About When We Talk About Love," which links horrible domestic abuse, alcoholism, despair, and violent suicide with *love*. It also mirrors the outcome of Carver's own dissipated life in a way that is encapsulated in a poem on his tombstone, displayed as the epigraph to the entire movie:

> And did you get what
> you wanted from this life, even so?/I did/And what
> did you want?/To call myself beloved, to feel myself
> beloved on the earth.

As the inner play within the movie, it mirrors the disintegration of protagonist Riggan's life even as he takes one last leap in the name of love, risking everything to direct and star in his first play on Broadway.[134]

The deeper layers of meaning that are embedded within the screenplay come into focus when we further compare its structure of "a play within a play" with that of Hamlet. Shakespeare has Hamlet direct the inner play while remaining an observer to that play. By watching the play as an observer in the audience, Hamlet hopes to summon up the courage to act in the way he knew he must. However, he fails to enact the image! In contrast, Riggan *both* directs *and* acts in the inner play, along with method actor Shiner and two others. There are several moments in the preview rehearsals, and then in the Opening Night, that give us a hint that the psychological distance maintained in Hamlet, which prevents the reality of the inner play from penetrating Hamlet's (or the audience's) consciousness, is dangerously breaking down in Birdman.[135]

During the previews, we see Shiner, the wild method actor, twice shattering the distance between play and audience, disrupting the plot and generating chaos: he breaks with the script on one occasion and attempts to really rape his "wife" on the stage in another. Furthermore, in the last preview performance, just before Ed, the Carver character (Riggan) is due to enter the final suicide scene, Riggan gets locked out of the theatre, has to walk around the building on the streets of New York in his underpants and wig, and is forced to make his entry through the audience. All these violent incursions from the inner play into the larger reality are met with shock, and then applause.

Finally, it's Opening night and Riggan knows in advance that Tabitha, an influential theatre critic is going to destroy his play, sending him back into artistic oblivion and financial bankruptcy. He decides to kill himself on stage at the ultimate moment when Ed, the Carver character, commits suicide. Riggan only manages instead to shoot his nose off, spraying blood into the audience.

An artistic breakthrough has occurred![136] Tabitha could not dismiss the performance. Instead she writes a rave review called, "The Unexpected Virtue of

Ignorance." This is a reference to Riggan's complete lack of experience in theatre, and how such ignorance (i.e. not knowing, uncertainty, leaping past traditional forms, *improvisation*—a point I will get back to) has led to a breakthrough in art. She acknowledges that a new art form has been produced—*ultra realism*.

Throughout the movie, on a larger scale yet, another breakthrough is threatening: a breakthrough into insanity! Birdman is Riggan's movie character, the one that made him famous as a screen star. Riggan became identified with Birdman, as did audiences throughout the Western world and beyond. The Birdman character is also a satirical version of the American eagle, ironically standing for everything that the USA triumphantly valorizes at this time.[137]

In the story, there were three movies of Birdman, all successful, and then Riggan's career was over. Riggan struggles to distance himself from the movie reality of Birdman and to have a real career as an actor. His efforts fail, and through the cracks in his personality, "the play that is Birdman" breaks through and disrupts the larger play that is Riggan's ordinary world—to the extent that, in the end, Riggan has only one exit—out the hospital window.

We once again see the mysterious meteor arcing across the sky but, equally mysteriously, we see Riggan's daughter running horrified to the window and then looking up, first in wonder, and then in delight. We are not shown her vision of things but we are left with the question: did a new art form, or way of being *happen*, out of the wreckage of Riggan's life, just as it apparently did with Carver, at the end of his life?

What is the nature of the possible *inception* or new way of being that takes place from deep within chaos, turbulence, disaster, disintegration, and violence, as shown in the movie? While the movie unsparingly portrays the collapse of an American way of being as configured and preserved in the symbol of that great bird of prey, the American eagle, it also suggests, on several scales of self-similarity, that, from within this apocalyptic end, an inception is taking place—one that has the status of an art form, one that has its source in love, as suggested in Carver's epitaph.

The hidden structure of "Birdman" is a fractal, an invisible strange attractor that is gathering to itself the chaotic disintegration of traditional art forms, shattered lives, and the way of being of an entire culture. This structure is the self-ordering principle that could engender a new form, an art form that is also a new way of being. We do not see this art form yet but one thing is clear. Its emergence will only come by way of death, as so clearly shown in the fateful moment when Riggan sees his *alter ego*, that soaring, shining star of American pride and ambition, finally bending his knees in humility before the same porcelain god that we each must submit to on a routine basis every day.

We are given a further hint of the quality of this new art form when we see an anomalous breakthrough occur on yet another, larger scale. The background score is played by a jazz drummer who suddenly appears twice *within* the play, once on the streets of New York where Riggan spontaneously throws some coins to him, and once in a rehearsal room of the Broadway theatre. This nod from Riggan to the jazz drummer whose music underscores the entire movie, suggests a dramatic acknowledgement of the singular importance of improvisation in a time of chaos where tradition and predictability are no longer possible guiding principles into the unknown future.

S TALKER

From the outset, you will need to bracket your prejudices with the word "stalker" appearing as the title.[138] "Stalker" has nothing to do with predatory or obsessional behaviors, i.e. stalking victims, like the movie Fatal Attraction, for example. The name here refers to smugglers, taken from the book this movie is based on.

In fact, to "get inside" this movie at all you will have to bracket most of your expectations about what a movie is supposed to do and be about. Stalker is considered one of the top 50 movies for all time (British Film Institute) and these accolades are probably due in large part to Tarkovsky's mastery of the cinematic medium.

I suspect that what I have to say about the greatness of the movie will not belong to the tenor of the general favorable criticisms of the movie. That is to say, my perspective on the movie does not focus on Tarkovsky's undoubted artistic mastery. I am seeking simply to say what the movie itself says to us, about itself, in its own terms. The sparse script, the camera work, the colors, the actors, all weave seamlessly together to say something to us, something essential that needs to be heard and I will try to say it. This means that I will not be offering any external interpretation of the movie's more enigmatic elements. I will stay within the "text" of the movie, as it were, and let *it* speak through its images, script, action, scenes, etc., to us.

For a moment, remove the script, which is sparse enough as it is; remove the sound and lighting effects which are used with the delicacy and precision of a Japanese tea ceremony master, and what do you see for over two hours? It's astonishing to realize that *all* you see is this—three middle-aged men stumbling around rather aimlessly in the bush land of a gigantic disused rubbish dump (the detritus of a bombed out or abandoned city), during which time nothing much happens! Literally!

At the end of the movie even the central character bemoans the fact that the journey was a failure, that nothing has changed after all his efforts to take his companions "somewhere". There are no murders, no fireworks, no breath-taking action scenes, no strange appearances of alien figures, and no buildup to a climax or resolution. I suppose we could make a tentative comparison to the style and mood of "Waiting for Godot." I thought also of a certain kind of modern men's group, where men go together into "the wilderness" in order to "find their authentic selves," the "wild man within," or to rediscover the living quality of nature or animal spirits, etc. At the heart of many such forays into nature is a desire to find *otherness* in some form or another, some light of intelligence other than the bright light of the ego that so dominates our ordinary perceptions today. Instead, many such well-intentioned journeys into the "interior" end up with lasting memories of male-bonding to be sure, but little else, in terms of the stated intention of encountering a living *other* whose light may eclipse that of the ego and truly initiate the human being into a new reality. In other words, although there may be some thrills and spills that are well worth remembering and recounting over a beer, often nothing *else* much happens in terms of relativizing the light of the ego in deference to a greater light or intelligence that wants to "speak".

Stalker can easily be seen this way, i.e. as a portrayal of three tired, disillusioned, middle-aged men, looking for meaning in an age of nihilism—a scientist, a writer, and a self-styled "group facilitator"—who manage to convince themselves that they are on a journey to encounter an "alien" presence called the Zone, somewhere on the forbidden outskirts of the burned out, destroyed husk of a city, in order to find its center, simply called the Room, where all desires will be satisfied. Stalker even persuades the other two men to pay him for his services. And so they embark on this quixotic journey (imagine Stalker as Don Quixote and his companions as Sancho) together for two hours of my time, a day of theirs, during which *nothing much happens!*

Why then, was I so gripped by this movie, from start to finish, hanging on every line of speech, every gesture, every mood that came and went? Why was I not disappointed for a second, during the many moments of high tension and expectation of disaster, followed by nothing much at all. Stalker expects some imminent and dangerous response from the alien Room whenever they make a supposed (according to Stalker's judgment only, by the way) wrong move, even though Writer or Scientist cannot see anything untoward about to happen, at any point on their quest. The expected devastating response never happens. The tension builds and then simply releases into ordinariness. No alien presence at all, no punishment, just a bush here, a mist there, a building, a tunnel—all perfectly ordinary and explainable! Why did I not feel let down or even betrayed when Stalker, at the end, weeps with his sense of failure to guide his companions into fulfillment:

They do not believe in anything. The ... organ with which they believe has atrophied! ... nobody believes. Not only those two. Nobody! Whom should I lead in there? Oh, God ... And the most terrifying thing is ... that nobody needs it anymore. And nobody needs that Room. And all my efforts are worthless!

This movie is structured masterfully, from start to finish, by ambiguity. And it is an ambiguity that can be "resolved" only by destroying the very essence of the movie's intent to build ambiguity and hold it in tension through the entirety of the drama. Only then, i.e. by holding this ambiguity without resolution, can something true appear—to us, the audience—through the errancy of our three protagonists.

The ambiguity is written into the script this way: Stalker is a humble psychopomp.[139] His wife knows he is blessed as "God's Fool." He knows the Way. Like Moses he can show the way to others but cannot himself enter the Promised Land where all desires are satisfied. He describes his role in a passionate outburst when Scientist reveals his clandestine purpose to destroy the Room with a bomb:

Yes, you're right, I'm a louse, I haven't done anything in this world and I cannot do anything ... And neither could I give anything to my wife! And I do not have any friends and I cannot have, but you cannot take what's mine from me! Everything is already taken from me, there, on the other side of the barbed wire. All I have is here. Can you understand! Here! In the Zone! My happiness, my freedom, my dignity — everything's here! For I lead the same [people] as me in here, unhappy ones, suffering. They ... They have no other hope left! And I—I am able to! Can you understand—I am able to help them! Nobody else can help them, but I, louse (shouts), I, louse, am able to! I am ready to shed tears of happiness that I am able to help them. That's all! And I want nothing else.

Psychopomp or delusional psychotic? Let's continue. What is the Way that Stalker knows? Keep in mind that the mood of the entire movie is one of end of days, apocalyptic, a civilization disintegrated, nihilism near its nadir. In one scene, for example, Stalker falls asleep with his companions and we hear the voice of his wife reciting what seem to be lines from Revelation:

And there an immense earthquake took place, and the Sun became dark as sack cloth, and the Moon was like covered with blood ... And the stars of the heaven fell to the ground as if a fig-tree, shaken by a great wind, let its unripe figs fall down. And the sky hid itself, rolled up as a scroll; and various hills and isles moved from their places (laughs)

The Way, then, is into the heart of hopelessness.

Stalker leads his skeptical (and gullible?) companions deeper into the "wasteland" through an eschatological landscape dominated by the presence of water in a variety of forms (mist, rain, wastewater, pools, streams, puddles, mud, wells, etc.) He uses a variety of methods that can only be called mantic practices: He insists that they must follow a path of indirection; that the Zone is maze-like, shifting all the time, and filled with traps; that it demands respect or else it punishes. He uses his intuition to find the right path by an oracular method of hurling a metal nut tied to a ribbon ahead of them, revealing the right way. He sees signs that no one else notices.

Natural events such as a wind rising, or a mist,

become warnings about mistakes but, and here is the other side of the ambiguity, in spite of Stalker's dedication and conviction, nothing ever happens. At one point he cries out in alarm that Writer has taken a wrong turn and now is lost to humanity, declaring at one point, "I never choose, myself, I'm always afraid. You cannot imagine how terrifying it is to make a mistake ... but somebody has to go first!"

Writer, however, turns up quite unharmed a few minutes later. All Stalker's actions are based on his conviction that the Zone is founded on an alien presence. Is Stalker on to something that no-one else notices, i.e. he is a true psychopomp, or is he psychotic, catching others up in his delusional system? There is simply nothing in the movie to confirm or disconfirm his perceptions of the present or future (e.g. go this way or die).

The Room is the center of the Zone and they finally arrive, according to Stalker anyway. Within an abandoned, gutted building is a doorway (threshold according to Stalker) to a waterlogged room with a big puddle covering the floor, filled with its share of litter and garbage. The puddle appears mirror-like until light rain disturbs the surface. The complete ordinariness of the scene is amazingly highlighted by an old telephone which suddenly rings. Scientist, seeing that it is working, uses the phone to call his colleagues back in the city telling them that he has the bomb and is going to use it, against their wishes, to destroy the Zone. He is doing this to prevent other people from being drawn to the Zone under false pretenses. He is completely rational about the Zone and its non-meaning. Everything we now see seems to support his and Writer's skepticism. But now he begins to have doubts:

We assembled it ... with friends, with my ex-colleagues. This place, as we can see, cannot make anybody happy. (punches in the numbers; assembling is over). If it falls into the wrong hands ... Actually, I do not know now. Then we realized ... that one shouldn't destroy the Zone. If it is ... If it even is a miracle, it is a part of nature, and it means it is a kind of hope, so to speak. They hid this bomb ... And I found it. The old building, fourth bunker. It seems there must be a rule ... one should never perform irreversible actions. I do understand, I'm not a maniac (sighs), but while this ulcer here is open for every scum ... I will neither be able to sleep or to rest. On the other hand, maybe the innermost will not let it happen. Ah?

Writer is more susceptible to Stalker's persuasions but he too now has a crisis of doubt asking Scientist:

... ah ... how do you know, that this miracle really exists? Who told you that dreams really come true here? Did you see anybody who would have been made happy here? Ah, maybe Porcupine (Stalker's mentor)? And actually, who told you about the Zone, about Porcupine, about this Room?

Scientist answers, "*He* did," meaning Stalker, and Writer concludes, "then I do not understand anything at all. What is the meaning to come here?"

Once the two men pass through their crisis of doubt, they notice how very quiet the Room is. Is it merely quiet or have they broken through to a realm of stillness, or Silence, the realm where all desires are satisfied? Is a greater light at last penetrating and eclipsing the light of their ordinary consciousness? Or is the mystery available only to Stalker, once again, leaving his companions in their benighted ignorance?

More ambiguity! They sit at the threshold and Scientist, being a scientist, cannot resist casually throwing stones into the Room and its puddle, maybe to see what happens. Nothing happens, beyond ripples.

Near the beginning of the movie, Stalker warns his companions that no one ever returns the same way they came and indeed, at the end, we are not shown how they return. The scene simply opens up at the same bar where they all first met. Nothing much has changed, it seems. Stalker believes the trip was a complete failure. Yet, in an extraordinary final scene, at Stalker's home, his daughter, thought to be a mutant cripple by others, begins to quietly exercise her mental power of telekinesis, moving glasses on a table, simply by looking at them.

Something now indeed *is* happening! What are we to make of this scene in the light of the entire movie's structure of ambiguity, where Stalker can equally be seen as a psychopomp and a delusional psychotic? Right from the beginning we are struck with the mood of nihilism and its anxieties of an epochal "loss of meaning." We also hear from Stalker that, in the end, "everything has its own meaning." The movie seems to be suggesting that to *make a decision* about meaning (three men stumbling around in a meaningless rubbish dump, or two initiates being led to a meaningful revelation by a psychopomp) is the wrong way. The Way may be to hold and sustain the ambiguity without trying to resolve it by a decision. Stalker offers us a "procedure" if you like, for holding this ambiguity:

When a man is born, he is weak and supple, when he dies he is strong and callous. When a tree grows, it is tender and gentle, and when it is dry and hard, it dies. Hardness and strength are companions of death; suppleness and weakness express the freshness of living. That is why what has hardened, will not win.

We can hold this ambiguity of private, subjective meaning (Stalker) vs. public general meaninglessness (Writer and Scientist), by becoming pliable, fluidic, rather than rigid and hard in our convictions or categories of thought. Stalker's admonition is resonant with the plethora of fluidic imagery in the movie: mists, wind, mud, and water in all the variations that I mentioned above. If we can remain fluidic in our attitude, then something, a "child," may be born out of that condition of ambiguity, something quite unexpected that, without even trying, has already surpassed what for us is an impassable barrier between spirit and matter, mind and body, literal and figurative, inner and outer interpretations, prosaic and poetic realities, etc.—all hardened categories of thought, easily overcome by a child.

Call it telekinesis if you like, but don't get too literal about it!

THE MAN WHO KNEW INFINITY

I'll begin with a synopsis:

After spending his time as a shipping clerk, Srinivasa Ramanujan (Dev Patel), a self-taught mathematical genius, gets the break he has been waiting for when G.H. Hardy (Jeremy Irons), an esteemed professor at Cambridge, takes him under his wing. Leaving his young bride to travel across the world to England, Ramanujan's journey is wrought with skepticism from Hardy's colleagues. But under the mentorship of the eccentric professor, Ramanujan finds the courage to prove the naysayers wrong and gain the respect that he truly deserves.

The film accentuates the contrast between two worlds: Ramanujan's pastoral homeland in India and the male dominated confines of Cambridge - with its fraternal codes and everyday politics within the faculty. Ramanujan, whose impetus towards creativity is spurred by intuition and spirituality, is utterly displaced in the western world, where mathematical theories must be rigorously and rationally backed by proofs. Through a slowly burgeoning friendship with Hardy, an institutional relationship slowly gives way to a deeper understanding, and Ramanujan's talents start to gain credence within the university, just as worsening health plagues him, and the country plunges into the first world war.[140]

A self-taught mathematical genius! What kind of "teaching" could this be? When Ramanujan finally reveals his secret to his Cambridge collaborator, Hardy could not believe it, and refused to believe it, being a dedicated atheist. Can any modern person believe it? Ramanujan said he *received* the formulas complete, from the goddess, claiming "to dream of blood drops that symbolized her male consort, Narasimha, after which he would receive visions of scrolls of complex mathematical content unfolding before his eyes." His long-time English colleague Hardy thought that the formulae were "arrived at by a process of mingled argument, intuition, and induction, of which he was entirely unable to give any coherent account." He (Hardy) also stated that he had "never met his equal, and can compare him only with Euler or Jacobi."[141]

Ramanujan simply spoke what the goddess told him. He had gaps in his knowledge of the various methods of mathematical proof developed laboriously in the West, and yet could deliver solutions to the most complex pure mathematical problems in the world. Hardy knew that, as brilliant as his Indian colleague surely was, nobody would accept his formulae unless he could prove them to the satisfaction of the skeptical (and envious) mathematical community at Cambridge. Hardy therefore set about teaching Ramanujan how to prove his formulae in the traditional way and so they collaborated until his work was acknowledged and he was accepted as a Fellow of Trinity College at Cambridge.

This review is not another celebration of genius, however. While seeing the movie I apperceived a "background" movement as reflected in the "text" of the movie, one that speaks to an urgent issue of our modern times. So while I will be using the language of the art form, I want to simultaneously say what spoke to me through the vehicle of the art form, i.e., this remarkable movie.

Hardy lamely describes the core of the phenomenon of Ramanujan's genius as inspiration mingled with argument and induction, lacking any coherent account. Yet Ramanujan's account is perfectly coherent when understood from within its terms, i.e. as a thought of God. Accompanying this self-presentational thought is a mood of devotion, surrender and humility, and a non-acquisitional attitude which we could call gratitude.

Ramanujan spent many years from about the age of ten learning the language of mathematics and this work prepared him (with the appropriate concepts) to become an adequate vessel for the inspirational message from the goddess, in the form of complete formulae that were independently verified by others.

Ramanujan's cultural practice of devotion to the goddess could not be understood let alone received by the Cambridge dons. He was forced to learn *their* accepted cultural practice, which is rooted in skepticism and the principle of falsifiability. There is a ruthless aspect to this kind of "testing the claims to knowledge," even a sadistic pleasure, in seeking not merely to falsify but to destroy Ramanujan's impertinent, unproven claims. This was portrayed so well in the movie. As a result of the onslaught of unmitigated attacks, Ramanujan's health began to fail.

Although medical reasons were found for his early death at 32 years old, the fact that Ramanujan was uprooted from his own culture, separated from his child-bride, and forced to assimilate uncompromisingly to another, alien, cultural practice that had nothing to do with love, submission, humility and gratitude—these facts are enough for me to conclude that Ramanujan was, in fact, killed.

A vessel for love is killed off! No one is to blame. It

is a matter of privileged cultural practices! Love and innocence are a deadly combination today, in a world ruled by Power. Ramanujan was inducted, if you like, into a modern culture that says, in effect: Oh, you think you can bring love *innocently* into our world. Well, let's show you what happens! And he was shown—envy, greed, exploitation, power, resentment, downright hatred, were all presented to this Innocent. Hardy, his only friend there at Cambridge had no idea of the human catastrophe in the making. His response to the attacks was to show Ramanujan how to toughen up: learn how to prove your results. They will listen to you. I will make them listen to you. He is right, of course, but he could not see the human price of such a demand. Ramanujan's results were greedily appropriated to the Western "Cause" (e.g. his formulae are being used to study Black Holes today) but nobody seems to have noticed the dead body, or to care how it got that way.

The speed with which the gift of love seeking entry in the world today is appropriated by power and/or destroyed by hatred is breath-taking. Yes we have the gold but the vessel has gone missing. Too bad, let's just go on with what we have and use it for our own purposes. No one asks if the goddess has another aim in mind i.e. other than exploitation by humans for their own purposes, in so gifting this young man Ramanujan with her exquisite formulae.

Does love have another *telos* in seeking incarnation through the human vessel?

We can get a clue from this profound movie. In one scene of his early life, Ramanujan describes his relationship to his inspirations. His passion and engagement with mathematics lay in a love of Form. Now, as it happens, I studied and taught mathematics and I know this kind of love. I could do algebra easily because it was never a matter of calculation for me but a matter of recognizing form. For example, I could apperceive the binomial form appearing from within the most complex arrangements of symbols.

It is beautiful!

Ramanujan could perceive this *beauty* of the mathematical world on a scale that only Euler and Jacobi could match. Beauty is love made visible in the phenomenal world, in this case, the world of mathematics. Suppose the goddess, or as we might say today, the *other*, wished to enter Creation through the vehicle of Ramanujan's psyche. He wanted only to serve and so love was able to emerge as Beauty in his chosen cultural practice of mathematics.

But what happens when this innocent love seeks to enter the modern material world as represented by Cambridge? It collides almost immediately with power and its institutional interests. Ramanujan met this force with no defences, and was destroyed by it. The level of hatred aimed at him and his "methodology" was portrayed in all its menace and destructive power. The damage went to his body and he died a year or so after becoming a Fellow of the Royal Society, at age 32.

You might say that beauty was ravaged where a being of love might have been created. Can you imagine what might have happened if Ramanujan had been received with human love and understanding and allowed to become the spokesman of love that he truly was? He could have initiated hundreds of students into the discipline of mathematics as a form of love *incarnate* in the world, displayed carnally as the real person, Ramanujan!

Hardy loved mathematics too, but his love was decidedly disincarnate. He lived in a world of Platonic Forms, an ideal world that pre-empted the human world of appearance and error—so much so that, for example, he could not relate to Ramanujan as a human individual. He barely noticed that Ramanujan was seriously ill and failed to notice entirely that British racists had beaten him up, leaving bruises over his face. There is a split in Hardy's kind of love. It is the split between a preferred ideal or perfect world of mathematical form opposed to a devalued world of appearance, now ruled by a power that can treat people brutally, without feeling. This split in the West killed Ramanujan.

What is the background movement that is "shining" through the text of this movie? Love is seeking incarnation into material existence. This "innocent" love does not know about the loveless, power-driven conditions of material existence today, even though this existence is love's creation. Keats put it exquisitely when he asked, and answered, the question, why this world of suffering or vale of tears: "Call the world if you please 'the vale of soul making' then you will find out the use of the world ... Sparks of the Divinity are not souls until each one is *personally* itself" (abridged).

For him, the world and its suffering and death is the agency that brings the pure and innocent intelligence into full incarnation as the transformed individual, who is now able to speak for love in the *real* world, even as it is today, so driven by the purposes of unfettered power. Ramanujan was crushed by this real world. Yes, his formula remain, abstract things of idealized beauty, to be used as tools by others, gladly. But the human vessel was destroyed and so love could not complete its descent into a personal soul-identity, i.e., the individual Ramanujan, as Keats says.

We lost a living incarnation of love in the realm of mathematics and only a living incarnation can initiate others into the realm of love in a personal, human way, so that actual humans begin treat one another lovingly, valorizing beauty over efficiency and utility in the pursuit of their chosen cultural practice, while at the same time being well-equipped to deal with the machinations of power in this world.

THE MAN WHO FELL TO EARTH

When I heard of David Bowie's passing, I recalled what for me may be my all-time favorite movie, The Man Who Fell to Earth (1976).[142] At that time I wasn't able to say how the movie moved me—I simply drank it in. It momentarily quenched a thirst that I did not know was there, being in my twenties at the time. Now, as I write this testimonial to a ground-breaking artist, I marvel at the fact that the whole movie is about thirst —a thirsty, dying world, and an emissary going out into the unknown to find the waters of life and replenish his home planet.

This emissary who has so much to tell us about the condition of his (our?) planet is poorly received. He is not believed, and instead is used for purely human ends. All effort is bent to normalize him and destroy his "alien" status. There is simply no interest in his being an alien, and what he may be speaking to us, as such. He resists the indoctrination process as long as possible, never losing sight of his mission—to find water and replenish a dying planet. His efforts fail and he finally drowns himself in loneliness and alcoholism. He writes a message, inscribed in a music album, intended to be sent "home", presumably to let his family know the extent of his efforts, and failures, but the message-bearing nature of the music gets lost and it becomes simply another music album to be sold for profit.

Is this the fate of David Bowie and all like him who shout the same message to us, about our psychic condition of "wasteland"? Is this the fate of his latest album and its alien message to us?[143] Yes, it has sold well, but will we hear its message? What would happen if we acknowledge the "alien" status of the emissary and, instead of normalizing him by explanation, or interpretation, we drank in his message in all its strangeness? When this alien wants to make love to us, and his skin begins to ooze the life-giving moisture that could restore water to our thirsty psyches, do we react with horror, recoil with disgust, or do we drink it in? If we accepted the life-giving essence of this "alien" moisture, then maybe, just maybe, we could then learn how to speak its watery language and its message could then, finally, "come home":

> Something happened on the day he died
> Spirit rose a metre and stepped aside
> Somebody else took his place, and bravely cried
> I'm a blackstar, I'm a blackstar

B Y THE SEA

What happens when you don't speak an unspeakable pain?[144]

A worn-out couple drives into a seaside resort. He is a writer who substitutes the bottle for inspiration. She is a former dancer in New York. Both were once the "toast of the town". Their boredom, their mutual distance, hides a secret which is growing like a poison in her body, slowly turning her mind. He, being a writer no doubt, pleads for speech. He knows what she needs to say, what the matter is, but she refuses to speak, preferring silence and a growing dependence on pills. He turns once again to the bottle.

Both are, underneath this veneer of "quiet desperation," very angry.

But the unspeakable pain insists on its own "speech" and if she won't speak it directly, it will show itself in other, more mysterious ways that, at first, baffle him. There is a small hole in the wall to the next hotel room where a young married couple are "getting pregnant" in as many ways as possible. She surreptitiously watches them and soon, he joins her. This little hole becomes a portal to their vibrant past. His intentions are fairly straightforward. Perhaps this voyeurism will awaken new life in them, now. Her intentions are much murkier, oblique, and less readable. He asks several times, "what are you doing," "what's this all about?" For example, she buys the young man a jacket that is identical to the one her husband wore when they were younger. So, when they peep through the hole in the wall he sees himself as a young man in the next room.

When he looks through the hole another time, he is shocked to see his wife getting undressed for the young man. It seems she wants to hurt him, and destroy the new marriage at the same time and, maybe, insanely, get pregnant herself by this younger man. What was a simply a portal to their past transforms so that the past, their past, comes forward in time and begins to poison the present as an anomalous intrusion. In one memorable line, the writer-husband claims that the past doesn't mean anything if you don't remember it. But, if the past is still alive in some sense, it can poison the present, if it remains unspoken.

One scene repeats throughout: a solitary fisherman goes out to sea at dawn, disappears, and returns in the evening to the inlet. She asks, how can you go out in the morning, come back at night, day after day, without losing your mind? What is it that we don't know? A potent question indeed, one that goes to the heart of the question of speaking the unspeakable pain! Being a writer, he is equipped to offer an answer. The fisherman goes out with the tide and comes in with the tide. He doesn't fight it.

She has been fighting the pain of losing a child, fighting the loss of being the mother of his child. So much loss, unspeakable pain, and she fought it all by going against the tide. The pain still speaks. After all, it is the stronger, but it must now speak through the medium of her unraveling mind in twisted gesture and symbolic action.

This movie is an eloquent, artistic presentation of what happens to us in our refusal of the speech of the living body, that body that speaks in pain, joy, or any of the other affectivities that constitute our lives as embodied beings. This living body *will* speak but our refusal to participate in that speech results in our minds unraveling and giving rise to an increasing cacophony of crazy gestures and actions.

It's all relatively simple. Turn to that living body; participate in its speech, no matter how painful. Return to the living body and give voice to *its* speech! At the present time, most, if not all, of our styles of language and cultural practices privilege the human will. We only get notice of a greater will, call it the will of the body or the greater Being, when pain leaves its calling card as a rude penetration into our familiar world. We so often seek only to remove the pain and return to "normal" but what would happen if we listened to the pain as a message bearer of the greater Being, and even better, developed a cultural practice that could bring that message into visibility?

AFTERWORD:
our forgotten animal being

Imagine the psyche and empirical reality as two sides of the same coin! Over a long period of time we have come to privilege empirical reality entirely as the reality. And we have collectively erased the psyche and its reality from our vocabulary and cultural practices.

The anomaly is an event that challenges the dominance of empirical reality. Psychic reality intrudes into empirical reality with the force of trauma—a terrifying experience. Yet, the emotion, along with the alien status of its thinking, constitute none other than the character of undivided Life, returning after thousands of years of exile form our culture. The anomaly serves notice that we are, first and foremost, embodied beings and as such we share a nature with the rest of the animals.

This final essay describes the incursion of the anomaly, in its character as "animal", into my life, leaving its message burned into my being and changing the course of my life.

During the 1980's and into the 90's I underwent what has popularly come to be called a spiritual emergency. This term is meant to name a psychological process that is essentially transformative, even though it may display psychotic features at times.[145] A major aspect of this process concerned my encounters with "animals". To give a flavor for the phenomenology of these encounters, I'll begin with some extended excerpts from my journals that are also included in my books already cited:[146]

One afternoon, David was taking a nap on the couch and suddenly "woke up" in the *in between* state. The familiar paralysis was upon him again and to his amazement, he was nestling in the arms of a sleeping giant brown bear. The sheer *presence* of this animal was overpowering. It invaded every sense. David was intoxicated with the damp pungent odour of the bear; he could feel every coarse fibre of its hair; he felt the enormous weight of its paws across his shoulders; he touched the razor sharp claws that extended inches out and which could rake his flesh with ease. It was *real* and yet

David knew he was in the *in between* place, where his consciousness was now interpenetrating with the bear's. He wanted to flee but instead lay quietly until his normal consciousness returned. When he did finally awake to the day, he knew that from now on he would have to take the bear into account with every choice he made. The bear was behind and around him and he was no longer alone.

On another occasion, after spending a social afternoon with a young woman, David returned home with tremendous heat once again racing through his body. Exhausted, he lay down and then:

"I am in bed aware that I am sleeping, yet awake. I feel something entering that feels dangerous. I feel the presence of an animal merging with me, co-extensive with my human form. I move into a crouch position on the bed. I feel rippling power arcing through my chest and my mouth elongates and my teeth are sharp and bared. A growl utters easily from my chest. Power and grace in the animal body yet I am still human, too. I am conscious of my human experience while at the same time I have entered an animal consciousness. The power I feel is exhilarating. I have never felt such freedom. It takes over my speech centres and growls a long basso note with consummate ease. In fact he enters my entire body. All my senses are now available to him."

And on yet another occasion, "The lion approaches and I become him and he becomes me. I can taste his/my fur on my tongue. Pungent scent fills nostrils. Loping along on the Savannah in easy long strides. Natives, people with dogs are coming. Casually, no fear, claws dig into bark and muscular thighs push up into the crackling branches of a dry tree. Dog comes, slips, yelps in fear and pain, and crashes down. The men come. They are talking about the lion, teaching the young ones about fear. Yellow eyes watch unblinking and rough tongue idly licks an immense paw of power."

These episodes are merely a sample of the many that were given me over twenty years. As with any spiritual emergency, if the human participant can survive the onslaught of living meaning, then, after a time, the "tsunami" abates and she is left beached and stranded in a strange land, having to cobble a new life together, with very little of her past life to guide her. I say this from my knowledge that a spiritual emergency is fundamentally directed towards the future—the unknown future! The individual is caught up in a transformation of the spiritual background to the appearances of the world. If the individual can successfully contain the enormous energies of transformation, she is in effect initiated into a new set of real appearances: the same world begins to appear in a new way and the task of the individual shifts from "simply" participating in a spiritual ordeal, to the lifelong task of sharing, or at least articulating her perceptions of new real contours of the world.

This latter task is by far the more difficult and I say this even after enduring twenty years of a nearly fatal engagement with apocalyptic energies. It is more difficult because, as I said, the spiritual emergency is "aimed" at incarnating the unknown future "in" the psyche of an individual. The initiate thus *becomes*, in a non-egoic sense, an aspect of that unknown future.

When this incarnation stabilizes, the individual is returned to ordinary life but not as she was before. She now becomes subject to strange inner promptings that stir her to act, to give voice to the being she has in fact become, the being that seeks to come into the world as the new contours of that world. This being *compels*, as it were, from out of the future, urging her to give shape to its longings in some cultural form.

The spiritual or psychic background, i.e. the hidden cause of the forms or contours of the world (the appearances) is at this time undergoing a transformation. We all feel it in the prevailing worldwide mood of alarm or imminent catastrophe. Individuals who are more open to the psychic background of this mood can get caught in its processes. If the being of the individual is strong enough to withstand the fury of energies that are released when the language of stable forms breaks down, then he or she can become a vehicle or mouthpiece for a new configuration—the unknown future. I say "unknown" because the transformation occurs at the deepest layers of the psyche—at a depth where the individual psyche and the world psyche "touch". A psychic deposit is left in the initiate's being when the transformative process is complete.

The individual now has a strong sense of duality existing within. On the one hand, I knew I had been through "something" and that I had returned to daily life, with memories of my life intact. On the other hand, I could sense a new being within who was awake for the first time.

I gave my first description of this peculiar experience in 1996. During an intense period of "poetic" inspiration, for one full night I experience:[147]

> Two streams circulate in me, contradictory, gathering power. I feel a crescendo as I am filled to bursting point. It all stops. Just stops. Utter stillness. I look out the window and notice the pale dawn emerging. There is a presence in me, awakening to the morning also. Beyond the fluctuations of my own mind, an *other* is stirring who perceives the morning as well. There is a kind of timeless quality, stillness beyond compare. A wakefulness, a "someone else" who is perceiving the glory of the morning, for the first time through my eyes, as well as myself who could see that it was a morning, ordinary like any other.

This new being is the unknown future incarnate and stabilized in the human psyche. My task, from that time forward, is simply to say what this new being shows me, through my senses that "he" uses to perceive the new contours of the world.[148] I had to find an art form to say what "he" perceives, as best I could, in as many ways as I could.[149]

My persistent and intense encounters with animal being over the years all shared a common phenomenological feature. They all involve the emergence of a psychic animal presence that "desired" to use my sensory system in order to perceive the world its way—the animal way. In no way did I feel that they intended to harm me (at least after some initial terrors). I was rather being "asked" to step aside and allow them to gain access to my sensory-nervous system so that they could experience the world their way (i.e. the bear way or the eagle way, etc.) through that *human* system.

Real animals of course perceive the world in their peculiarly animal manner, but my experiences taught me that our animal being, the being that we share with real animals, seems to want to come to consciousness i.e. conscious of its own manner of perceiving the world. To do this it must enlist the consciousness of its highest representative, the human being. I think I am saying here that animal being is beginning to become conscious, through the agency of the prepared human being.[150] I have struggled for years to find the right way to say this and this struggle has served notice that the worldwide apocalyptic mood is a sign that the human being is undergoing a transformation in the definition of its essential nature.

A new configuration is called for from the depths of Being, one in which human consciousness and animal being are becoming united in a way yet to be languaged.[151] This is the unknown future. It appears that animal wisdom needs us in order to become conscious of itself and we need animal wisdom in order to break the devastating effects of our own excesses on the world—these power-driven excesses only made possible as we increasingly freed ourselves, psychologically at least, from those "eternal" regulating principles.[152]

It may well be that we are called from the depths of Being itself to this task of bringing the regulating powers of the world into self-consciousness, not merely for the sake for humanity, but for the sake of Being itself which seems at this time to be approaching terminal state.[153]

In the years subsequent to my ordeal I have devoted the remaining years of my life to the task of "saying what I am shown" by animal being and refining the art form that can carry such speech. I consider myself a poor mouthpiece in this regard but nonetheless I keep trying.

I will conclude this essay with an early attempt to say what I know needs to be said. We *are* being approached by animal being, after centuries of its systematic exclusion from all our cultural practices. Animal being now wants to perceive the world *consciously*, *as animal being*, not as interpreted by human rationality which, over the centuries, has offered interpretations of Life, based on hatred of our animality, conceiving it as non-spiritual, etc. With this increasing separation from animal being, as I have said, we have are freed, we believe, from any regulating principle, and thus capable of destroying Being itself—an incredible outcome of accelerating human excess.

Here now is my "poem" of the coming guest, the unknown future:

MERMAID
crowd gathers
centering young woman
struggling to walk
tune of derision mockery
only a cane to help her legs
so long and slender
curving stretching down
feet ending
strangely bending toes
no one knows her

where does she come from?
dark hair damply hanging
long shoulder sloping
brave souls addressing
song breathing from her lips
brave souls retreating
crowd offers more distant observations
such strange musical notes
escaping her mouth
moved to silence at first
distant memory stirring
bells water
tinkling against stone
tones
uncanny echoes blue depths
long forgotten by mankind
but among men

this beautiful silence of possibilities
so quickly filling

with known safety of fear
rock found

passing hand to hand
air suddenly cracking tight
rope pulled hard.
i am pulled too

but towards her

in that moment i see
eyes blue-gray reflections
sky upon water

hair windswept waves
legs strong lean
awkward hurting
toes not deformed at all
transparent skin webs

more used to a friendlier touch
than what hard ground can offer
voice echoing another world we once knew

now left far behind
love welling in my heart
music filling

penetrating

awakening dormant knowing
gentle tinkling sea bells
deep moans of leviathan

forming words within me
emerging from deep immersion in her
seeing rock raised to throw
stepping forward

crowd giving way
wave parting
stop! can't you see?

she is not crippled
she is a mermaid
a mermaid
mermaid
she is not seeking alms or favours

she is seeking . . . us

listen to her

listen
i have come! have come! come!
greetings! i have come!

A BOUT THE AUTHOR

I hold a doctorate in Consciousness Studies (1999). My thesis concerns the theme of "the end of the world", based on my own personal experiences lasting twenty years. At first it seemed to me that I was undergoing a purely personal psychological crisis but over time I discovered that I was also participating in the historical process of a transformation in the life of the psyche, as reflected in the enormous, even apocalyptic, changes occurring in our culture. During this difficult period of my life, I wrote two books: Living in Uncertainty Living with Spirit and Poems of Making, Poems of Death, as I tried to give voice to the meaning of my experiences.

My next three books, Mouthpiece, The Imperative, and Hearing Voices, explore the meaning of "the end of the world" more fully through an autobiographical approach. My subsequent books, including Animal Soul and Manifesting Possible Futures, establish a firm theoretical ground for the claim that the psyche is urging us towards the development of new inner capacities that can help us face the uncertainty of modern life and, as well, address the unknown future.

My book, Overcoming Solidity, continues this exploration in terms of our current structure of consciousness and its correlative world of empirical reality. Making New Worlds begins the work of articulating an art form that is emerging in response to the unknown future. I develop this theme more fully in The Coming Guest and the New Art Form. I have also written an unusual book, UR-image, which tells a story of four friends whose lives are interrupted by an anomalous intrusion of four possible futures, while

Oblivion of Being is a story of three friends participating in a transformation of being. Since then I have written The Peril in Thinking and Speech of the Unknown Future.

A preview of all my books is available on YouTube:

https://youtu.be/DKfiR_K5nps, or you can visit:
http://www.amazon.com/author/johncwoodcock

I currently live in Sydney with my wife, Anita Hansen, where I teach, write, and consult with others concerning their own journey through the present "apocalypse of the interior", as it has been called, in my capacity as a practicing Jungian psychotherapist. Anita and I also work with couples in a therapeutic setting.

Contact: jwoodcock@lighthousedownunder.com

END NOTES

1 Orwell, G. 1984. St. John: Brawtley Press, 2014, 49-50.

2 Pinker, Steven. "The Mystery of Consciousness". TIME. January 29, 2007, Vol. 169, 5, p. 59ff.

3 Ibid. 62.

4 Ibid. 62-69

5 Ibid. 62

6 Wolfe, Tom. Wolfe-Sorry-But-Your-Psyche-Just-Died. Othodoxy Today. [Online] 1996. [Cited: 07 23, 2009.] http://orthodoxytoday.org

7 Ibid

8 Ibid

9 Ibid

10 Op. Cit. 70

11 Op. Cit.

12 Op. Cit. 62

13 Both quotes—Freud, S. Totem and Taboo. NY: Moffat, Yard and Company, 1919, 207, 231

14 Lewis, C. S. Studies in Words. Cambridge : Cambridge University Press, 1967

15 Pinker: Op. Cit. 62

16 Ibid

17 Simons, Ilana. "The Literary Mind" in: Psychology Today. [Online] [Cited: 08 17, 2011.] http://www.psychologytoday.com/blog/the-literary-mind/200911/why-do-we-dream

18 Lewis, C. S. That Hideous Strength. London. Harper Collins, 2005, 353-355

19 Pinker: Op. Cit. 118-9

20 Woodcock, John C. Transformation of the World. Bloomington : iUniverse, 2009

21 See "Language and Cultural Form" in: Woodcock, John C. The Imperative: CreateSpace. 2015

22 Jensen, F. & Mullen, S. (1982): C. G. Jung, Emma Jung, & Toni Wolff: A Collection of Remembrances. 77. Cited in Hayman, R. (2002): A Life of Jung. 384.

23 Jung, C. G: CW Vol. 11. Par. 140. Shadow-work is thus a psychological process of overcoming the logic of exteriority so that we begin to perceive the real phenomenon in question as no longer so alien to oneself, but as something to do, psychologically, with oneself. This is the initial discovery of immanent relations, the very definition of shadow work i.e., what I felt to be so utterly other is, as psychological fact, "me"!

24 Ibid.

25 The Dark Knight, 2008

26 The Factor: Dec 16, 2015. https://www.youtube.com/watch?v=p1pYqgVT5As

27 See my UR-image for example—a story of four friends who encounter the vortex.

28 I have also received the image of vortex and tree as belonging together. See my book, Oblivion of Being.

29 Most likely this is an autonomous unconscious process that Trump has no idea about.

30 See my latest book, Speech of the Unknown Future for a discussion of this process. When the representational nature of language is lost then a being only exists as measured, "mapped," abstracted, etc. Otherwise it simply does not exist for us. Abstract language becomes reified, as my Professor at the debate on Iran so eloquently demonstrated.

31 Hubert Dreyfus. "Heidegger's Ontology of Art" in A Companion to Heidegger. Dreyfus, R. & Wrathall, M. (eds).

32 "The Origin of the Work of Art" in Off the Beaten Track. J. Young & K. Haynes (eds). Cambridge University Press, 14.

33 PD-US, https://en.wikipedia.org/w/index.php?curid=3740793

[34] Stephanie Rosenthal, artistic director for the 20th Biennale, Sydney.

[35] The Annunciation of the Virgin Deal: http://www.mca.com.au/exhibition/grayson-perry/

[36] Heidegger calls "things" and equipment, in terms of their respective modes of being: the "occurrent" or "present-at-hand" and the "available" or "ready-to-hand".

[37] That is, thought or the mind is positivized, substantiated, like external reality—hence virtual reality (virtually the same). The movie, The Matrix exemplifies this interpretive move.

[38] Heidegger refines this reality as our technological world, to distinguish its appearances from that of previous historical epochs.

[39] As Dreyfus says through his metaphor of the illuminated room (see p. 2).

[40] The Coming Guest and the New Art Form

[41] https://www.youtube.com/watch?v=316AzLYfAzw

[42] Owen Barfield (1957). Saving the Appearances, London: Faber and Faber, pp. 145-146.

[43] Thinking, like music, does not exist except as thought by us or performed by us, yet neither are products of our subjectivity. This is negative "objective" reality!

[44] "objective" in quotes because the reality of psyche is "pure" interiority or inwardness, i.e. beyond the inner/outer disjunction that has dominated our thinking and culture for thousands of years.

[45] See, for example, my essay The Coming Guest: fountain-mouth at: https://www.academia.edu/22365927/THE_COMING_GUEST_Fountain-Mouth

[46] Wind, E.: Pagan Mysteries in the Renaissance. New York: Norton, 1968, 238.

[47] Ibid

48 In what follows, I draw several quotes and many words and phrases from Richard Rorty's book, Essays on Heidegger and Others, v2 (1991). Cambridge University Press.

49 Wikipedia

50 Op. Cit. 5

51 Ibid. 158

52 Ibid. 157

53 Ibid. 4

54 Ibid. 155

55 Ibid. 34

56 Rorty, R. "Heidegger, Contingency, and Pragmatism" in A Companion to Heidegger [Dreyfus, R. & Wrathall, M. (eds)] 2005. Blackwell Publishing. Kindle edition. Loc 9391

57 Op. Cit. 88

58 Ibid. 103

59 See my postscript.

60 None of what follows was calculated or deliberate. I followed the flow of imagery as the geyser came up.

61 Wikipedia

62 I realize this is a complicated statement. Perhaps "rational mind" or "reflective mind" is a useful qualification here.

63 Wikipedia

64 The Exceptional and the Normal: what can we learn from extreme states of mind.

65 See: One Apple Film Festival

66 See my book, The Imperative, for the complete dream, which shows the initiatory process that can take us through to another future. Available at Amazon.

67 My books are primarily an attempt to make these transforming experiences available to others.

68 See my book, Poems of Making Poems of Death. Available at Amazon.

69 The body that can participate in initiations is essentially different from the modern empirical body. Our modern bodies no longer are transparent to spirit and so, initiation scarification for example no longer carries a "message" from Being, but has become simply a cosmetic tattoo.

70 This is most evident with the explosion of performance-enhancing drugs.

71 When a relative of mine found a breast cancer, we were handed a standardized treatment manual not unlike, in its rhetoric, a car manual.

72 There are many formulations: self/other; inner/outer; subject/object; psyche/soma; spirit/matter; I/not-I; psyche/world, etc.

73 Robert Bosnak: Embodiment: Creative Imagination in Medicine, Art, and Travel. New york. Routledge, 2007. 20.

74 Robert Bosnak - Embodied Dream Imagery in Therapy, Medicine, and the Creative Process. Found at http://jungatlanta.com/store/dreams.html

75 See my books, The Imperative and Mouthpiece for my accounts of these experiences. Available at Amazon.

76 Quotes around so many words indicate ambiguity in meaning; they are not to be taken literally.

77 CW 18. The Tavistock Lectures, Lecture II. See notes p. 65.

78 C. G. Jung Letters. V2, 43.

79 CW 16. Par. 343 ff.

80 His book, De humani corporis fabrica is "the most significant work in the development of modern medicine and anatomy. Vesalius' "radical skepticism", as he described it, led the young, headstrong anatomist to challenge the old ways and examine the human body with his own hands and eyes. His resulting anatomical tome propelled science into modernity." Found at: http://www.vesaliusfabrica.com/en/original-fabrica/medical-history.html

81 This arrangement is the logical basis for the efficacy of magical practices.

82 This logical structure accounts for how working magically with a body part like fingernails or hair *could* have an effect of casting a spell on the victim.

83 Ibid, 2.

84 Ibid, 6.

85 Ibid, 7.

86 Ibid, 8.

87 Ibid, 16.

88 Ibid, 14-15.

89 See above full quote in C. G. Jung Letters, op. cit.

90 I suggest earlier that his choice was aided by a temporary dip into an earlier logic of appearances, so that he could perceive the identity between Latin words and their resemblances in reality.

91 Owen Barfield: The Rediscovery of Meaning. San Rafael. The Barfield Press, 1977. 171 ff.

92 Ibid, 172

93 As we could when the logic of resemblance prevailed.

94 For a more complete and detailed discussion, see my essay: The Hidden Legacy of The Red Book in Thomas Arzt (Hrsg.): Das Rote Buch. C. G. Jungs Reise zum "anderen Pol der Welt" Studien zur Analytischen Psychologie, Bd. 5, Königshausen & Neumann, Würzburg, Germany, 2015. Also found at https://www.academia.edu/12876153/Hidden_Legacy_of_the_Red_Book

95 Jung recorded his experience of suspension throughout The Red Book and the text expresses the new reality he incepted. See my essay, op. cit. for a fuller discussion of the meaning of "suspension".

96 Ibid.

[97] See C. G. Jung Letters, V2: 590: "Who is the awe-inspiring guest who knocks at our door portentously?"

[98] "Composed by the Side of Grasmere Lake"

[99] Bortoft, H. (1996). The Wholeness of Nature. Aurora. Lindisfarne Books.

[100] The term, "historical imagination" is from Owen Barfield and is a method of participating with past consciousnesses.

[101] Old Norse kalla "to cry loudly;" Proto-Indo-European base *gol- "to scream, shriek." From WordBook. (2012).

[102] From the psyche's point of view, the "past" means "psychic depth", or the depths of our being.

[103] Paul de Man, reading Nietzsche, asks: "are the axioms of logic adequate to reality or are they a means and measure for us to create the real ..." de Man, P. (1979). Allegories of Reading. New Haven. Yale University Press. 120.

[104] Rilke, R., Barrows, A. & Macy, J. (tr.) (1996). Book of Hours. New York. Riverhead Books.

[105] _____ Leishman & Spender, S. (tr). (1967). "The Ninth Elegy" in Duino Elegies. New York. Norton.

[106] For a fuller account of this period of my life, see Woodcock, J. C. (2015). The Imperative. CreateSpace.

[107] Eliot, T. S. The Wasteland.

[108] I had this dream-vision c1995.

[109] "Human beings ... are so deficient in the essentials of bush education such as having a proper sense of smell and hearing ..." From van der Post, L. (1978). A Story Like The Wind. New York. Morrow.

[110] Our present cultural practices reflect a definition of human beings as isolated centres of consciousness over and against a material world whose meaning can only be posited by these centres of authority—if we don't endow the world with this or that "world view" then the world holds no meaning at all.

111 My book, Oblivion of Being, narrates a story of three friends who, following an inceptive moment, engage in the effort of developing a new cultural form that can reflect a transformation in the definition of the human being and world.

112 Jung, C. G. (1951) Synchronicity: An Acausal Connecting Principle in CW Vol 8, par 826 ff

113 Ibid, par. 827

114 Time magazine: 1/12/1975: https://jungcurrents.com/synchronicity-and-the-death-of-jung

115 Jung, C. G. Op. Cit. par 827.

116 Ibid.

117 https://rsarchive.org/Search.php?q=toads

118 https://www.academia.edu/17626867/Living_In_Uncertainty_Living_with_Spirit

119 Avatar (2009).

120 Quoted in The Telegraph, UK> http://www.telegraph.co.uk/culture/film/film-news/6977817/Avatar-fans-suicidal-because-planet-Pandora-is-not-real.html

121 The Girl with the Dragon Tattoo (2011).

122 Lewis, M. The Big Short: Inside the Doomsday Machine. NY. Norton, 2010. The Big Short movie (2015).

123 This way of understanding is, as Nietzsche says, "to be able to express something old and familiar."

124 Elliott, J. Unexpected Light: Travels in Afghanistan. London. St. Martin's Press, 2011.

125 The story of the corruption in credit ratings companies is a book in itself.

126 Lewis, M. Op. Cit. 10.

127 Heidegger: The Age of the World Picture

128 Lewis, M. Op. Cit. 245.

129 Ibid. 247.

[130] Ibid. 225.

[131] I call the new structure: the interpenetration of fictional and empirical reality, although this naming itself does not language the new reality in its own terms. See the foreword of my book, UR-image, available at: https://www.academia.edu/12915773/UR-image_Foreword or at Amazon.

[132] Oblivion of Being. Available at Amazon.

[133] Birdman (2015)

[134] Riggan is the movie protagonist, who previously starred as, and becomes identified with, a comic book hero—Birdman.

[135] Another appearance of the anomaly (fictional reality penetrating into empirical reality).

[136] An anomalous rupture breaking down the distance between audience and play.

[137] The American eagle in its predatory stance is the symbol that gathers all the current practices of American society and gives meaning and coherence to all its cultural activities.

[138] Stalker (1979). With appreciation to Kirill Zimin for the translation of the movie script at: http://tarkovskyzone.proboards.com/thread/87

[139] Psychopomp: one who grants safe passage for psyches to the after life, Hermes is a psychopomp, as are dogs and cuckoos, both of which appear throughout the movie.

[140] The Man Who Knew Infinity (2015). Synopsis found at http://sgiff.com/browse-all-films/man-who-knew-infinity/

[141] https://en.wikipedia.org/wiki/Srinivasa_Ramanujan

[142] Died Jan 10, 2016.

[143] Blackstar (2015)

[144] By The Sea (2015)

[145] See my books, The Imperative and Mouthpiece for my biographical account of this time.

146 I used my pen name of "David" to gain some distance from the raw material which was still, at the time, "white hot" and overpowering, even in recall.

147 My book, Poems of Making Poems of Death emerged from this period.

148 Heidegger demonstrates that the *essence* of language is saying as showing. See his On the Way to Language.

149 This effort of finding the "right" art form is in my judgment more difficult than going through the ordeal, as awful as that is.

150 The prepared human being is the one willing to undergo a breakdown of the categories of thought that separate us from ours and the world's *animal* being, i.e., to go through the end of supremacy of the "Cartesian" ego as the only source of subjectivity in the universe.

151 This call is one of desperation as our excesses now threaten Being.

152 Jung understood that the great animals in the background (i.e. the psychic background) are the regulating principles of the world. See C. G. Jung: Letters, V2. p. 605.

153 With the very real looming possibility of non-being!